war

medals

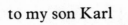

to my son Karl

war
medals

Derek E. Johnson

Arthur Barker Limited
5 Winsley Street London W1

acknowledgements

To the Chief Librarian, Mr T. A. Baker,
A.L.A., and his staff at the Clacton Public
Library for all the assistance during my re-
search. Also to Lt-Col D. A. Johnson, Director
of Public Relations (Army), and to the HIAG
Organisation, Western Germany.

Thanks are due to H. Hoffman for permission
to use the photographs on pages 6 and 63; the
British Museum for the photographs on pages
11–13 and 112–18; Coins Magazine for the
photographs on pages 14, 15, 30, 45, 58, 59,
70, 82–4, 90–105, 108 and 126; David Pitcher
for the photographs on pages 16, 40, 47–57
and 67; and Stan Shelley for the photograph on
page 62.

Copyright © Derek E. Johnson 1971

SBN 213 00308 2

Printed in Great Britain by
C. Tinling & Co. Ltd, London and Prescot

contents

Hermann Göring, World War I air ace wearing his *Pour le Mérite* or, as it has become known in collecting circles, 'The Blue Max'

introduction

I can think of no other hobby that actually brings the history of so many battles and feats of individual gallantry into one's own parlour than that of collecting war medals.

Battles that have long been forgotten by the general public spring readily to mind when each individual piece is closely inspected. For on ..early every medal struck, be it the very first official medal for Waterloo, or those of the 1914–18 War, one can find the number, name, rank and regiment of each and every man who participated. We can be swept from one continent to another at the twist of a medal; from that 'thin red line' of Scots, whose cool daring at Balaclava has only been equalled by the Charge of the Light Brigade during the Crimea, to those days of the Zulu War and the ensuing heroism of Rorke's Drift. Once into the South Africa War which saw Britain out of Victoria's reign and into that of Edward VII, such famous names that still prick the memory like Baden Powell, founder of the Boy Scout Movement and Winston Churchill are to be found linked with many a daring escapade. Here also the advent of modern firearms called for a different type of fighting and battle tactics with 'Tommy Atkins' forsaking his colourful red and blue uniform for that of a more drab khaki hue. One outstanding feature of this war was that two medals were issued, one for Queen Victoria, who died in the middle of the conflict in 1901, the other for the new King, Edward VII.

Not to be forgotten are the medals of the Imperial German

Forces who swept all before them in the Franco-Prussian War of 1870–1 and the South West African War of 1904–6. The so-called war-to-end-all-wars, 1914–18, only really succeeded in bringing about the downfall of the Kaiser and the loss of 7,494,186 lives during one of the bloodiest wars this modern world has ever known. A much coveted award of this war is the *Pour le Mérite* or, as it is known in collecting circles, the Blue Max, a medal which became closely associated with those German fighter pilots flying their new-fangled flying machines. Some of these men used the skies as a duelling ground, sending a challenge to their English counterparts for an early morning showdown over the trenches. It had been known for them to abandon the use of the machine-gun in favour of their pistols! As with all such rarities these awards are commanding high prices and the novice must be on his guard against forgeries and 'doctored' pieces. There are many to be found, ranging from those of the reign of Elizabeth I to the more modern medals of Nazi Germany. A chapter on how to detect some of these 'interesting' items has been included. Rather than learn the hard and expensive way it is far better to join one of the historical research societies. Here, one can meet and exchange views on all aspects of medal collecting, be it the humble fire-fighters' award or the grandiose awards of State or Empire. For on most of the committees there are members of some of the world's leading museums – all specialists in their own right.

The whole adventure of collecting medals is really in the hunt. For nothing whets the appetite more than to find a much sought-after medal lurking in a box of junk in a bric-à-brac shop or at a church bazaar. All the better if one can purchase it for a few shillings and it turns out to be worth much more.

Some collectors shy away from medals without their ribbons, but here again being a member of a society will soon overcome this problem, for many members have access to hitherto unknown supplies and they will gladly sell a small portion for a copper or two. In a nutshell it boils down to three main points: learn by reading and handling; never pay a lot for a medal unless you know what you're about; and last but not least get to know your fellow collector and discuss medals till the proverbial cows come home!

1 short history of how war medals evolved

Even back in the primitive days of Man's beginning we find savage hordes bestowing awards upon one another for acts of bravery in battle. To this day we find tribes in Central Africa and the Amazon carrying out practices that were in vogue the world over centuries ago. Shrunken heads, scalp-locks and ears – these are really nothing more than a form of medal, being a mark of esteem and a badge to exhibit. Just a matter of saying, 'I was there!'

Medals as such can be traced back to the ancient Egyptians and Romans where plaques of brass or copper were awarded for outstanding feats of bravery. As these awards were sometimes cumbersome and weighty for personal adornment they ended up as part of the horse equipment, hence the presence of our ever popular horse brasses. During the Middle Ages a warrior, knighted on the field of battle, was permitted to carry a square instead of a swallow-tailed pennant and likewise to use a war cry, from whence we can trace the origin of the Coats of Arms.

Awards as such seemed to fluctuate with different monarchs. We find that one instance of a lower rank benefiting in such a manner was a Sergeant Weems of the 1st Royals, who, during the battle of Sedgemoor (6 July 1685), served the great guns with such verve and tenacity he was bestowed with a gratuity of £40.

Among the first medals to be officially recognised and to be classed as such are those awarded by Queen Elizabeth I after the defeat of the Spanish Armada in 1588 – but, then again only to the leading officers.

These were struck in gold and silver and had rings and chains for suspension, probably from the neck.

Although they are priced well out of the average collector's pocket whenever they appear upon the open market, one must never give up hope as such items do appear from time to time concealed in the odd box of junk at a local jumble or auction sale.

Once again, during the reign of James I, we find a medal almost identical to that of Elizabeth which is known in collecting circles as the 'Ark-in-Flood' medal. There are two kinds of obverse to this medal, one of which has a portrait bust of the King in armour with a ruff, and the legend FIDEI DEFENSOR encircling the head. This apparently was for military officers and the other, bearing an obverse with the King's head surmounted by a broad-brimmed hat, for his courtiers. There are various schools of thought on this point and historians and collectors are unable to agree as to what is what. The motto on the obverse of the second type is JACOBUS · D · G · MAG · BRITA · FR · ET · HI · REX; and on the reverse is an ark within an oval band containing the motto PER VNDUS SEVAS TRANQVILLA.

Charles I is recognised as having established military medals for actual military prowess. They were, according to the order of the Court, held at Oxford on 18 May 1643, 'to be delivered to wear on the breast of every man who shall be certified under the hands of their commander-in-chief to have done us faithful service in the forlorn hope'. These medals were only, as can be seen, given for very distinguished conduct in the field.

One bore the Royal image on the obverse and Prince Charles on the reverse; the other the bust of Charles on the obverse with the inscription CAROLUS · D · G · MAG · BRI · FR · ET · HIB · REX, and on the reverse the Royal Arms with the Garter bearing the motto HONI · SOIT · QUI · MAL · Y · PENSE.

The two medals were struck in silver and are oval in shape, their sizes being 1.7in. by 1.3in., and 1.5in. by 1.2in. respectively.

The first recorded award of a medal for conspicuous conduct in the field is that made to an Irish commander who distinguished himself at the battle of Edgehill – the first battle of the Civil War, 23 October 1642 – by recovering a Royal Standard and important military equipment. The soldier in question, who later became Sir

Robert Welch, was presented with an oval gold medal specially cut to the King's instructions by the Royal 'graver of seals and medals', Thomas Rawlins. This medal, ordered by the King on 1 June 1643, bore on the obverse his own figure and that of his son Prince Charles, and on the reverse a facsimile of the banner Welch saved at Edgehill, together with the legend PER REGALE MANDATVM CAROLI REGIS HOC ASSIGNATVM ROBERTO WELCH MILITI. Encircling the royal busts was the inscription CAROLUS REX MAGNAE BRITTANNIAE FRANCAIE ET HIBERNIAE CAROLUS PRINCEPS. The medal, oval in form, was 1.7in. by 1.5in.

Oliver Cromwell, that puritanical tyrant dubbed 'Lord of the Fens', was, by and large, instrumental in forming an army with a 'new look'. He laid the groundwork for an army that was uniform in weapons and dress with strict regulations concerning discipline. Death was the order of the day for drunkenness, being absent without leave, losing weapons, blasphemy and wasting powder. On the other hand he always paid his men regularly and on time. He was a hard man when dealing with his adversaries as can be seen in the case of the 5,000 men he had put to the sword after the battle of Drogheda in Ireland. One good thing that did come out

11

Dunbar Medal 1650 (obverse and reverse)

of Cromwell's reign was the first campaign medal which was awarded to officers and men alike. Although not strictly a medal as recognised today – this one being suspended by a chain from the neck – it was to be one of the first medals awarded to all ranks. The Dunbar medal, as it is known, was struck on 3 September 1650 to commemorate the defeat of the Scots Royalists at Dunbar.

Designed by that famous medallist, Thomas Simon, it was struck in two sizes. Gold specimens, measuring 1in. by 0.85in., were for officers and silver ones, 1.35in. by 1.15in. for other ranks. On the obverse of this medal we find the bust of Cromwell in armour with the inscription in a semi-circle above WORD AT DVNBAR THE LORD OF HOSTS SEPTEM Y3=1650. The reverse shows an interior view of the House of Commons. Bronze medals do exist but the reverses of these are plain.

Once back under the rule of Charles II there is no record of military medals being struck. Likewise during the reign of James II, William and Mary, and Queen Anne, although naval medals were issued to commemorate victories over the Dutch, while in the reign of the latter a large silver medal was struck, apparently for the Navy.

The reign of George I reveals nothing in the form of a medal, and in the reign of George II there appear to be only two – one for the battle of Culloden (16 April 1746), where the Duke of

Cumberland well earned his nickname of 'The Butcher', and the other for taking Louisbourg in Canada on 27 July 1758, where after a seven-week siege, the French garrison was forced to surrender to General Amherst.

It was the Honourable East India Company who set the vogue in 1766 by awarding a medal to their native officers who had quelled a mutiny among European troops at Morighyr, and again in 1778 and 1792 against Hyder Ali and his son Tippoo Sahib. Although these were not official or Sovereign awards, they are much sought after and when they do appear upon the open market command a good price.

It was during this period that certain high-ranking British naval officers decided to have medals struck privately as awards for their own men. These were usually copies of their own official awards but struck in bronze, pewter, tin or lead. As booty was the driving force behind any battle in that day and age, it really depended upon the value of the find as to which type of medal the recipients could expect to receive.

It was after the battle of Waterloo, when Great Britain and her allies finally defeated Napoleon, that the first official war medal was struck – the 1815 Waterloo medal. On the obverse it bore the head of the Prince Regent and on the reverse a winged figure of Victory seated on a plinth, the base bearing the word WATERLOO. This medal was suggested by the Duke of Wellington, and his

top British War Medal 1914–20 (obverse and reverse)
bottom 1914–19 Victory Medal (obverse and reverse)

below left 1948 Pakistan Medal (obverse and reverse)
below right Dutch Silver Flying Cross 1941

name can be found around the top circumference. An outstanding feature regarding this first war medal is the instructions issued when awarding it – 'the ribbon issued with the medal shall never be worn but with the medal suspended to it'.

From this period onwards we find medals struck for nearly every engagement. Some countries followed Great Britain almost at once, whilst others utilised former Orders and decorations

15

struck for the nobility and made them into lower-grade awards as war medals.

Thus we come in a full circle, from a period of no medals at all, through the many battles that went to forge the Empire, through two World Wars, Korea, Malaya and Aden, to the minor skirmishes in Suez, Hong Kong and Ireland. Now we must look to the heavens for our limited astronautical awards for if there ever was a Third World War we would surely blow ourselves beyond the realms of anything so earthly as a medal!

2 different types of material used

Medals as such can be found in a vast variety of materials from the beautiful creations struck in the Orient to those cast in lead or tin awarded to the Sikhs and Sepoys while serving and fighting for their British masters. In many instances they evolved from awards bestowed upon the King's champions in the form of mansions, horses, swords, muskets or priceless gems captured from the baggage train or treasure ship of a vanquished enemy. In Imperial Russia up to 1917,* it was the practise to award certain high-ranking officers the Order of St George and the 'Golden-Sword' with a diamond-studded scabbard and the badge of St George mounted on the pommel. The sword knot or tassel was the same colour as the medal ribbon, being gold with three black stripes.

Gold medals were awarded to high-ranking officers from before the times of 'Good Queen Bess' together with silver awards for junior officers. A few remaining examples of these medals can be viewed in the British Museum, although many dubious 'Armada Medals' are found offered for sale from time to time.

Examples of bronze medals struck from captured enemy cannon can be witnessed in the case of the British Victoria Cross (Crimea cannon), the German South-West Africa medal, 1904–6, and the British Star for Kabul-Kandahar, 1880.

Tin and lead medals were not only restricted to the native troops

* This practise was still in vogue under Hitler's Third Reich where honour daggers were awarded to SS, Luftwaffe and U-Boat officers for deeds of outstanding merit and valour. A U-Boat commander's dress dirk given by Admiral Dönitz on 9 May 1944 sold for over £250 when put up for auction in 1966. It is believed that only six such daggers were made and presented by Admiral Raeder and to date the one presented by Dönitz is the only recorded example left.

employed by the British in India and the Colonies, for the Turkish troops fighting in the Gallipoli Campaign were awarded a cheap tin-plated, very crudely finished star, which after cleaning once or twice reveals the true metal beneath. This is also true of the medals issued by France, Germany and Great Britain after the 1914–18 War. Only in this instance the gilding is upon brass or iron which is all very well if they are only lightly cleaned, but if an over-zealous polisher starts to work he will end up with a two-tone medal!

From the ancient Empire of China we find exquisite examples such as the Order of the Double Dragon, worked in gold and enamels with a blue cabochon jewel mounted in the centre; how different from the plastic/brass accolade conferred upon the heroes of North Korea and the Viet Cong.

Although medals of the Soviet Union are rather austere and sober in design there are examples worked in silver, platinum and diamonds awarded to high ranking USSR officers, with others in gold and silver.

With true Germanic thoroughness the Order of the Deutsches Kreuz was not only struck in gold with brilliants; gold and silver; and silver; for wear with the dress uniform, it was also faithfully copied in gold and silver braid for second-best, and in silks and cottons for battle-tunics! The collector is also likely to find a variety of one particular kind of medal struck in different types of metals and dies. One example being the black, silver, and gold wound badges of the Third Reich which, during the early part of the 1939–45 War were struck in heavy metals but towards the end they appear in very thin alloy with a hollow back to them. This is also true of the medals and badges of Italy during the reign of Benito Mussolini, which seem to lack substance and detail even from the start. The same yardstick can be applied to the medals of Great Britain after World War I where the well-designed pieces of Queen Victoria and Edward's Empire seem to melt away overnight to be replaced by unimaginative cupro-nickel awards for World War II.

Now with man walking around on the Moon's surface it won't be long before they start to award medals for daring exploits in space. The mind boggles at trying to imagine such a medal nestling amidst the average collection and at what one would have to pay for such an award.

3 fakes and forgeries

how to detect wrong rivets, bars, names, enamels, etc.

As in all realms of collecting we find the heinous work of the forger close at hand. Not only does the novice suffer, for with all the modern methods of science to be utilised the pieces that are struck stand up to the closest scrutiny and have indeed even baffled the experts. In fact a number of pieces have been purchased by museums and have only been discovered to be fakes after the market had started to be swamped by similar 'rarities'!

Greed is the mainstay of the forger and while they can spend countless hours perfecting a copy of say, the *Pour le Mérite,* they cannot expect to turn these out by the dozens and stay undetected. Far better for them to stick to the Iron Cross, Merit Cross, Air Crew Europe Star and Russian or American awards, which can be passed off to most dealers for between £1 and £1.50. There are countless numbers of such forgeries appearing all over the world, some good – too good in fact – others being rather crude and shoddy. I have had journeymen 'knockers' show me small cases of such medals, not just the odd one or two but in lots of a dozen or more. If you do have any doubts about that fellow in the pub who will sell you one of Himmler's medals for a couple of pints, beware! The chances are you have become the proud owner of a copy. The only sure way is to deal with a reputable, well-established firm backed by years of handling the genuine articles.

It may seem odd that the case of faking medals far superior to their genuine counterparts could ever arise, but in the case of the Air Crew Europe Star this has actually happened. While this award is exactly the same as the other World War II Stars it has become rather scarce over the last year or two and is consequently fetching £5 to £6.

However, whereas this medal resembles the original Air Crew Europe Star in nearly every way it falls down by being too finely finished. All the other World War II Stars have rough, sharp points to their edges but in the case of the copy it has polished points which the forger in his over-zealousness has seen fit to adjust. Just how rough the original medal was finished can be judged by the following anecdote. I have a former Guard's military tailor bring me the odd medal or two whenever he is sorting out his old boxes of equipment, and while we were discussing this question of fakes he recalled when, just after World War II he was engaged on the task of stringing and mounting groups of medals. He and his assistant finished the day with fingers split and bleeding caused by these rough cast Stars. In fact they were so rough that the Canadian Government refused to issue the standard British war medals to their servicemen and struck their own. These are the same as the British issue but minus rough edges.

Most of these fakes or re-strikes are cast by the lost-wax casting method where every detail is copied faithfully when moulding. With the old method of sand casting one was left with a medal not only slightly oversize but filled with minute pock-marks, all too evidently a fake. Nowadays, with the lost-wax method, apart from being slightly undersize these medals are really hard to detect. In the case of the Air Crew Europe Star the mounting for the suspender ring is 0.85in. thick, while on the lost-wax casting re-strike it measures approximately 0.80in.

Iron Crosses for both the First and Second Classes have also been appearing upon the market over the past few years. Struck from the original dies these are quick to spot as they appear too brilliant and tawdry – rather akin to the cheap seaside jewellery sported in amusement arcades. Just lately however, the metal is being artificially aged to such perfection that some of the leading arms and armour auction rooms have included the following statement in their catalogues: 'Owing to the large number of Nazi uniform and accoutrements being used for films, television and plays, it is becoming increasingly difficult to ascertain the authenticity of certain pieces. We catalogue all Nazi items believing them to be genuine unless otherwise stated.'

Whereas on the Imperial and early Nazi awards there is a small number stamped on the suspender ring, towards the end of the war this was omitted. Nazi medals and awards in general also carry the official ringed RZM or DRGM stamp. Once again I can only echo the old adage: 'When in doubt, don't!'

It stands to reason that if a *Pour le Mérite* is offered to you at a bargain price you wouldn't think twice about purchasing it providing it looked right enough. Looking all right however is not enough in this day and age of the clever forger. The last 'Blue Max' that I heard being sold as a bargain (£25) turned out to be a clever re-strike, and took five medal experts at one of London's leading museums to finally pronounce it a fake. They *knew* there was something wrong but couldn't quite put their finger on the fault. That was until one of them inspected the enamel more closely. It was here that they found the vital clue. As I have previously mentioned, when the lost-wax method is employed there is a slight loss of thickness in metal, not really enough to notice on an ordinary medal but when there are colons between the inscription and then enamel as well something has to be lost. In this case it was the tiny colons that lost their heads; when the enamel was applied they were covered over completely, thus supplying the museum authorities with that vital clue.

There is no end to this faking business be it making the actual medal itself or just adding or removing certain bars to convert it into another prize piece. Even antique awards are not all that they seem to be. Forgeries of the Elizabethan Naval Medal and the Mysore Campaign (1791–3) medal have been discovered but as these have been cast in sand they bear all the typical characteristics of such pieces. The latter was a poor class of medal in any case, being struck by a Calcutta silversmith using a very bad die indeed – leaving the counterfeiter little or no trouble in copying it. On some of these medals the sepoy shown has five cannon-balls at his feet, while on others there are only two. To recognise these fakes one rarely has to use a spy-glass to pick out the sand holes and grains scattered over the medal's face. On some, work has been attempted to remove these marks with a chasing tool but even these are easily spotted once one knows what to look for.

When one is dealing with the 'Bar Changer' it is rather more difficult to establish the authenticity of such a piece, for unless one has copies of the Medal Rolls at hand or has made a close study of the regiment involved, it proves something of a problem to state categorically that the medal has been tampered with. Close study of the rivet mountings can usually give a hint of any adjustment, because unless the proper tools are used in removing and replacing these small round-headed silver rivets they tend to bend or burr over.

While we are on the subject of suspenders, bars and rivets, I think now is the time to clear up the misconceived notion regarding the first general official war medal, the 1815 Waterloo. Although it is a well-known fact that this medal was originally issued with a one-inch large steel ring, through which the $1\frac{1}{2}$-inch (sometimes two-inch) ribbon passed, collectors and dealers sometimes think that unless it still retains the steel clip and ring it must be a doctored piece and therefore of no value. This, however, is not the case, because as this was the first official medal the authorities had not taken into consideration the amount of wear it was going to receive if, as laid down in Standing Orders, 'the ribbon issued with the medal shall never be worn but with the medal suspended to it'! The clip which held the ring in position proved to be rather weak and as a result the possessors of the medal frequently had suspenders made to their own pattern. These are to be found in all shapes and sizes – they were made in silver or steel, and range in workmanship from that of a top silversmith to the regimental farrier.

The naming of medals is yet another field that the forger strays into for it could be in the regimental naming alone that certain medals become of any value. Although all Waterloo medals command a good price one named to the 27th Regiment is very rare and specimens have been found to be renamed from time to time. Once again it is rather difficult to arrive at a firm decision over the type of lettering used on these old medals because before the use of a machine press these names were engraved by hand. Many have the name spelt wrong mainly because they were engraved in foreign parts where the local craftsmen could hardly understand the Queen's English, let alone write it! On the Waterloo medal the lettering is very bold and left little margin between the edge of the medal and the top and bottom of the letters. On other early campaign medals the name could vary from very small tall Roman capitals to slightly sloping squat Roman letters, or then again there are examples engraved in a neat round hand. The only sure way to establish the authenticity of such a medal is to compare it with others of the same award or take it to one of the societies or museums listed at the back of this book.

Although there are far too many examples of fakes, re-strikes, copies, call them what you will, to be listed here I have set out a few known examples that are being sold as the genuine article, as follows:

Imperial German Iron Cross 1st Class
Imperial German Iron Cross 2nd Class
Imperial German *Pour le Mérite*
Nazi 1939 Iron Cross 1st Class
Nazi 1939 Iron Cross 2nd Class
Nazi 1939 Wound badges in black, silver and gold
Nazi 1939 Silver Merit Crosses with swords and without swords, pin or screw back
Nazi 1939 Brass Merit Crosses with swords and without swords, hung from a ribbon
Nazi Knight's Cross of the War Service Cross with crossed swords, gilt
Nazi Knight's Cross of the Iron Cross
Nazi Knight's Cross of the Iron Cross with oak leaves
Nazi Spanish Cross in silver with swords
Nazi Russian Front medal
Nazi War Order of the German Cross, gold border
Nazi Medal for Spanish Volunteers in Russia
Nazi Bar to the Iron Cross
Waterloo medal and renaming of same
Kimberley Star (the genuine ones have a hallmark which includes the date – the letter 'a', for the year 1900)
Crimea medal: bars and renaming of regiments
South Africa, Queen's: bars and renaming of regiments

Air Crew Europe (complete re-strike)
Soviet Russian Order of the Red Star Breast Badge
Russian Defence of Leningrad 1941–5 medal in bronze
Russian Order of Glory, 1943, 2nd Class in silver
America Air Medal
America Medal of Military Merit (Purple Heart)
British Military Cross

Even as I compiled the data for this chapter I heard of many such forgeries appearing upon the market; once again I can only stress the point regarding arming yourself with as much knowledge as possible before parting with that hard-earned cash. There are one or two good weekly and monthly magazines appearing on the British market now which novice collectors should quickly avail themselves of.

4 a selection of world medals

Russian medal for Hungary 1849

Awarded to Russian soldiers who took part in the Pacification of Hungary at the request of Austria in 1849, this medal bears on the obverse the Russian double-headed eagle, surmounted by a crown, having a shield on its breast, encircled by a collar and badge, containing the figure of St George and the Dragon. The eagle to the left is holding a baton in its claws, and the one to the right a globe with a cross above it. Above, the radiated Eye of Providence; encircling the whole, in Russian characters, GOD IS WITH US: HEAR O YE PEOPLE, AND SUBMIT, FOR GOD IS WITH US. On the reverse, also inscribed in Russian characters, FOR THE PACIFICA- TION OF HUNGARY AND TRANSILVANIA, 1849. It is a small circular medal with plain, raised double borders and was struck in silver and bronze.

French Médaille Militaire

Founded in 1852 by Louis Napoleon, when President of the French Republic, this is the French equivalent of the British Distinguished Conduct Medal. Struck in silver and just one inch in diameter, it is formed of a close band of laurel wreaths, encircling on the obverse the gilt bust of Napoleon facing left, with his name in gilt letters on a blue enamelled band. On the reverse, the wreath encircles a narrow band of blue enamel which borders the gilt centre bearing the legend VALEUR ET DISCIPLINE. The medal is surmounted by the French eagle, with outspread wings, and is suspended from an orange-coloured ribbon with green edges.

It is interesting to note that after the Crimean War, Louis, then Emperor Napoleon III, presented this medal to five hundred British non-commissioned officers and men who had distinguished themselves during the campaign.

In 1870 the design was changed with the gilt female head of the Republic replacing the head of Napoleon, and a trophy of arms consisting of swords, muskets, crossed cannon, a cuirass and an anchor replacing the French eagle. The inscription reads REPUBLIQUE FRANÇAISE* 1870* and on the reverse VALEUR ET DISCIPLINE. The ribbon is yellow with green edges. Within the past few years the '1870' has been omitted.

French Croix de Guerre

Established in April 1915 this medal was to commemorate individual mentions in despatches. It was struck in form of a bronze cross *pattée* with crossed swords running through the angles. The centre bears the female head and inscription REPUBLIQUE FRANÇAISE.

Up to 1939 the ribbon was coloured green with seven thin red stripes, after this date the centre remained green with three red stripes together with thicker red edges.

The Cross is awarded to all ranks and bears the distinction of the different class of despatches by the following emblems worn on the ribbon. Army Despatch – small bronze laurel branch (*Palme en bronze*); Army Corps Despatch – silver gilt star; Divisional Despatch – silver star; Brigade, Regimental or similar Unit Despatch – bronze star.

There can be no mistaking the kind of action a winner of a *Croix de Guerre* will have encountered for every mention is represented by its emblem, for a man can wear the Cross with the bronze palm and silver star. After being awarded five bronze palms, a recipient is entitled to wear instead a silver palm.

Garibaldian medal 1860

This medal was given to the Garibaldians in Sicily by the Municipality of Palermo, and distributed to the troops by

Garibaldi on 4 November 1860, in the square in front of the Royal Palace, Naples. It was not recognised by Royalty, however, until 1865. On the obverse, within the words AI PRODI CUI FU DUC GARIBALDI is a spread eagle standing on a scroll, on which are the letters S.P.Q.R. Below are three stars, all in relief. On the reverse, outside a circle of laurel leaves are the words MARSALA, CALATA-FIMI, PALERMO, and within the circle, IL MUNICIPIO PALERMITANO RIVENDICATA MDCCLX. In the exergue is a star. This small circular medal, 1⅕in. in diameter and having a plain, raised double border, is suspended by a silver loop and ring from a crimson ribbon with narrow yellow edges, on which is attached the Arms of Sicily in silver, bearing the words UNO DEI MIL.

Papal States Campaign 1860

This medal was given by Pope Pius IX to his troops, including the Irish Brigade of Volunteers, who served under Major O'Reilly against Garibaldi. It was issued in gold to officers, and in silver and white metal to privates.

The obverse takes the form of an open ring formed by the body of a serpent – a symbol of eternity – on the head of which rests an inverted cross; around, on a plain band with the simple, moulded edge is the motto, PRO PETRI SEDE ▲ PIO · IX · P · M · A · XV ▲ . On the reverse, in the band, VICTORIA QVAE VINCIT MVNDVM FIDES NOSTRA*.

This is a circular medal, 1½in. in diameter, with a plain, raised double border. It has a scroll bar and claw clip suspender, and hangs from a crimson ribbon, with two white stripes, edged with yellow.

Russian Caucasus medal 1859–64

Granted by Emperor Alexander II for services in the Caucasus this small silver medal 1 1/16 in. in diameter bears on the obverse his bust in profile facing left, and on the reverse across the centre the dates 1859–64 encircled by an inscription in Russian characters stating that it was awarded for the subjugation of the Western Caucasus.

There is also a bronze, with crossed swords between the arms, to be attached to the uniform by means of a ring and bar attachment, which was awarded for the same campaign. It bears the explanatory inscription across the horizontal arms and Alexander's initial in a Russian character surmounted by the Russian Imperial crown in the upper arm, and the date 1864 in the lower arm. In the circle which occupies the centre is the Russian eagle.

French medal for Franco-Prussian War 1870-1

This bronze medal was awarded to the survivors of the Franco-Prussian War and as such is a very artistic medal. It is somewhat larger than the usual French military award and bears on the obverse the helmeted and armour-clad bust of a woman, with the legend REPUBLIQUE FRANÇAISE. The reverse has a finely arranged trophy of French arms, supporting the French tricolour, and a panel inscribed AUX DEFENSEURS DE LA PATRIE (To the defenders of the country). There is a small suspension ring and the ribbon is green with four black stripes.

French St Helena medal 1857

It was to be over fifty years before a medal was struck by Emperor Napoleon III and awarded to the survivors of the great army of Frenchmen who had served *le petit Caporal* during his campaigns from 1792 to 1815. This oval, bronze medal has on the obverse a beaded circle with laurel leaves, which frame the whole medal and the laureated head of Napoleon facing to the right with the legend NAPOLEON I EMPEREUR. On the reverse, within a beaded circle, is the inscription A SES COMPAGNONS DE GLOIRE SA DERNIERE PENSEE STE. HELENE 5 MAI 1821. (To his companions in glory his last thought St Helena 5 May 1821), and around CAMPAGNES DE 1792 A 1815, with a small five-pointed star beneath. The French Imperial Crown, standing above the oval, has a ring affixed to the top through which a $1\frac{1}{2}$in. wide, green with narrow stripes, ribbon passes.

The British, for their part glad at last to be rid of this thorn in their side, had the East India Company issue a halfpenny with the Arms of the EIC on the obverse, and a laurel wreath enclosing ST HELENA HALFPENNY, 1821, on the reverse. Although the British strongly denied the rumours that this coin was nothing else but a warped way of saying farewell to the Emperor, the fact remains that this was the one and only coin to be ever issued for the island of St Helena.

French Légion d'Honneur

Proposed by Napoleon Bonaparte on 15 May 1802 when he was First Consul, the Order of the *Légion d'Honneur* was to be awarded for military and Civil Services.

The original Badge or Cross consists of a white enamelled badge with five double rays with silver balls on the points, resting on a laurel and oak wreath, tied at the base, and surmounted by an Imperial crown attached to the badge by a loop and ring. It has a ring for suspension from a crimson-corded ribbon $1\frac{1}{2}$in. wide.

The obverse has a silver-gilt radiated centre, upon which is the laureated head of the Emperor Napoleon, facing right, surrounded by a blue enamelled band, with gilt borders, inscribed in gold letters NAPOLEON EMPEREUR DES FRANÇAIS. On the reverse there is also on a silver-gilt centre of horizontal lines, the French Imperial eagle, surrounded by a blue enamelled band, with gilt borders, inscribed HONNEUR ET PATRIE, with a sprig of laurel below.

The Order was originally divided into three classes – Légionnaires, Grand Officers, and Commanders. After the Coronation of Napoleon (14 July 1804) the first class of Grand Officers was divided into Knights of the Grand Eagle (as the highest) and Grand Officers. There are five classes of the Order: Knights of the Grand Cross, Grand Officers, Commanders, Officers, and Knights.

The Cross for the Knight is in silver, and for the other classes in gold and of a larger size. The Knights and Officers wear it at the button-hole or on the left breast; the Commanders round the neck. The Grand Officers wear besides, upon the right breast, a silver Star, similar to that of the Grand Crosses; and at the button-hole the Cross in gold. The Knights of the Grand Cross wear a similar golden Cross, but larger, suspended by a ribbon across the right shoulder towards the left hip; and also, on the left breast, a silver Star.

The Star is of silver, similar to the Cross, without the wreath, having rays between the angles, and in the centre, within a band inscribed HONNEUR ET PATRIE, the Imperial French eagle.

Later the head of Napoleon was replaced by the laureated female head symbolic of the Republic, and surrounded by the legend REPUBLIQUE FRANÇAISE, 1870. On the reverse in the centre are the crossed French flags, surrounded by the motto HONNEUR ET PATRIE. In place of the French Imperial crown which acted as a suspender on the original badge or cross is an enamelled wreath. Within the past few years the date '1870' has been removed.

The Legion of Honour is the highest accolade of the French Republic and is awarded for gallantry in action or for twenty years' distinguished civilian or military service in peace. When awarded for war services the Legion of Honour and the *Croix de Guerre* are presented simultaneously.

USA Purple Heart

This decoration was first instituted by George Washington when he was Commander-in-Chief of the Continental Army during the Revolutionary War. In the true sense of the word it was not originally a medal, but a heart cut out of purple cloth or silk, edged with narrow silver braid.

Although one of the oldest American awards the Purple Heart fell into disuse after the Revolutionary War with the records showing only three men having won it during that period.

However, steps were taken some two hundred years later to reinstitute this coveted award and the following order was published on 22 February 1932, by the War Department: 'By order of the President of the United States the Purple Heart, established by George Washington at Neburgh, 7 August 1782, during the War of the Revolution, is hereby revived out of respect to his memory and military achievements.'

The regulations governing the revived decoration authorize awards as follows:

'For acts or services performed subsequent to 22 February 1932, the decoration is authorized to be awarded to persons who, while serving in the Army of the United States, perform any, singular meritorious act of extraordinary fidelity or essential service.'

On 19 September 1942 it was announced by the War Department that the Purple Heart would be awarded to all USA personnel killed or wounded by enemy action during World War II without distinction of rank. The award was made posthumously to military or civilian personnel who were killed while serving in any

Borneo Inauguration Medal 1965 (obverse and reverse)

Ghana United Nations Medal for Congo 1957 (obverse and reverse)

capacity with the Army, and to all those wounded providing they necessitated medical treatment. In December 1942 a further announcement stated that commanders of hospitals and other medical units were authorized to award the Purple Heart and Oak Leaf Cluster to United States soldiers wounded in action. This order ensured that wounded soldiers would receive their awards in the field of battle or as soon as they entered hospital. The Oak Leaf Cluster is granted to a man previously wounded who has already received the Purple Heart, while any soldier receiving severe frostbite whilst actually under fire also merits the award of this decoration.

The modern version consists of a heart-shaped medal, its face bordered in light bronze and a centre of purple enamel. The reverse is bronze and bears the inscription FOR MILITARY MERIT. On the obverse is a relief bust of General Washington in the uniform of a General. The Washington coat of arms is incorporated in the ring which attaches it to a purple ribbon, edged with white.

Croix de Guerre L.V.F. (Légion Volontaire Française)

Classed as one of the rare medals of the world is the *Croix de Guerre L.V.F.* which was authorized on 18 July 1942 by the Vichy Government in France (1940–4). Awarded to the French Volunteer division who assisted Germany in the war against Russia, it is struck in bronze with the French shield superimposed upon the German eagle on the obverse, while the reverse has the words CROIX DE GUERRE LÉGIONNAIRE.

The ribbon is green with black edges and seven narrow black stripes in the centre. Although it is thought that only four hundred of these crosses were ever awarded, fakes are known to exist.

Ordre National du Travail

Instituted by Marshal Pétain, the Vichy Premier, on 1 April 1942, this Order was to have consisted of three classes – Commandeur, Officier, and Chevalier. The reverse has the 'Francisque Gallique' badge surrounded by the words ORDRE NATIONAL DU TRAVAIL. On the obverse is a shield bearing the head of the Marshal encircled by the words PH. PÉTAIN MAL DE FR, CHEF DE L' ÉTAT, and surrounded by a wreath of laurel. The ribbon was blue with a red stripe at each edge. It is on record that no more than two hundred Chevaliers were ever appointed.

USSR Order of Alexander Nevsky
This Order was awarded to commanders of regiments, battalions, units and platoons for showing initiative in choosing the right moment for a sudden outright attack on the enemy and for infliction of defeat with minor losses of manpower; also for operational air attacks, leading up to a severe defeat of the enemy, and ensuring the complete success of a general military operation.

The badge is a five-pointed star in red enamel resting on a ten-pointed silver background, with radiating rays. The head of Prince General Alexander Nevsky is in the centre on a circular ground with his name in Russian. Each side of the centre portion are sprays of laurel joined at the bottom by a small shield with the hammer and sickle. A pair of crossed battle-axes appear above. The service ribbon is pale blue with a red central stripe. The Order, established in July 1942, has only one class and is worn on the right breast.

USSR Order of Glory
Instituted in November 1943, this Order was awarded to NCOs and rank and file of the Red Army and for junior officers of the Red Air Force who distinguished themselves in battle by being first to enter enemy positions or who by some act of personal bravery contributed to the success of the operation, by capturing an enemy standard or saving the standard of their unit, accounting personally for from ten to fifty enemy soldiers, disabled not less than two enemy tanks with anti-tank guns or from one to three with stick grenades or saved the life of a commander in battle at the risk of their own. There are three classes of the Order, and recipients are promoted automatically. The badge of the 1st Class is in gold; the 2nd Class is in silver with a gold centre; and that of the 3rd Class in silver. The Order takes the form of a five-pointed star, the centre design showing the Spassky Tower and the Kremlin, with two sprays of laurel and the word 'Glory' in Russian below on a red riband. The decoration is worn from a ribbon of orange *moiré* with three black stripes.

USSR Order of the Patriotic War

Yet another Order instituted during World War II as an award to those showing great heroism and courage in fighting off the enemy. There are two classes. The 1st Class is awarded to all ranks of the Red Army, Red Navy, troops of the People's Commissariat of Internal Affairs and guerilla groups who displayed courage, staunchness and gallantry in combat.

The Order of this class consists of a red star, bearing the hammer and sickle in gold with a crossed sword and rifle superimposed upon a golden sun-burst.

The 2nd Class is awarded to those who by their actions contributed to the war effort. The insignia of the 2nd Class is identical but silver instead of gold. Both bear the words PATRIOTIC WAR in Russian on a white band encircling the hammer-and-sickle emblem. The Orders are worn on the right breast and the service ribbons are 1st Class – red *moiré* with a central stripe of light red; 2nd Class – red with lighter red edges.

USSR Marshal's Star

Awarded solely to Marshals of the Soviet Union, artillery, aviation, and tank and mechanised troops, this award is a five-pointed gold star with a smaller five-pointed star studded with diamonds in the centre. The star of a marshal of the Soviet Union, in addition, has mounted, between each ray of the star, a large diamond.

The Star is worn around the neck, and the ribbon for marshals of the Soviet Union is red *moiré*, light blue for marshals of the air, gold colour for marshals of artillery, and claret colour for marshals of tank and mechanised troops.

USSR Order of the Red Star

Created in 1930 for officers and men of the Red Army, Navy, or Air Force, or units thereof, or institutions, undertakings, or social organisations performing conspicuous services in the defence of the USSR either in war or peace.

The Order consists of a red star, in the centre of which is a soldier of the Red Army armed with a rifle and bayonet. In a circle round this 'Ivan' is the inscription WORKERS OF ALL COUNTRIES, UNITE! Beneath it are the Russian initials 'CCCP' (USSR), and the sign of the hammer and sickle. The star is worn alone on the breast, but there is a service ribbon of dark red *moiré* with a central stripe of grey.

USSR medal for Valour

Awarded to service personnel of all ranks for personal bravery, this medal consists of a red and white enamelled disc figuring a tank and aeroplanes with the inscription FOR VALOUR, USSR. The ribbon is light grey *moiré* with blue stripes at the edges. Not only does the recipient receive a pension of ten roubles a month but has the right of free travel on the tramways.

USSR medal for Distinguished Service in Battle

This medal consists of a red and white enamelled disc with crossed rifle and sword and the inscription FOR DISTINGUISHED BATTLE SERVICE – USSR. It is awarded to military or civilian personnel for distinguished services in a battle area, and carries a pension of five roubles a month and free travel on the tramways.

The ribbon is light grey *moiré* with yellow stripes at the edges.

USSR 'Defence', 'Capture', and 'Liberation' medals

LENINGRAD

This depicts three soldiers with rifles at the ready position, behind a tower, and encircling all the words FOR THE DEFENCE OF LENINGRAD. Ribbon is olive green with a narrow dark centre stripe.

STALINGRAD

This shows five soldiers facing left with rifles at the ready, posed in front of the Red Flag, with the inscription in Russian FOR THE DEFENCE OF STALINGRAD. The ribbon is olive green with a narrow red centre stripe.

MOSCOW

The centre design is a tank outside the Kremlin. Below, a wreath and above the words FOR THE DEFENCE OF MOSCOW. The ribbon is red with three olive green stripes.

SEVASTOPOL

This medal bears the profiles of a soldier and sailor – the arms and flukes of an anchor below, with the inscription FOR THE DEFENCE OF SEVASTOPOL. The ribbon is olive green with a narrow deep blue centre stripe.

ARCTIC

A design covering all aspects of the services with a soldier in winter uniform; in front of him a tank; behind, a warship; above, aeroplanes. The inscription reads FOR THE DEFENCE OF THE SOVIET ARCTIC. The ribbon being of three broad stripes, of light blue, light green, light blue separated by narrow white stripes, and narrow white edges.

CAUCASUS

Surrounded by an ornamental border is a mixture of aeroplanes, oil wells, tanks, and a mountain. The inscription reads FOR THE DEFENCE OF THE CAUCASUS. The ribbon is olive green, with blue edges and in the centre very narrow stripes of blue, white, red, green, red, white and blue.

ODESSA

This depicts a sailor and soldier marching to the left, below, a wreath, and above, the inscription FOR THE DEFENCE OF ODESSA. The ribbon is olive green with a narrow light blue centre stripe.

KOENIGSBERG

This medal takes the form of a radiant star with a branch bearing five leaves and the words FOR THE CAPTURE OF KOENIGSBERG. The ribbon is green with three black stripes.

BERLIN

Yet another star with a half wreath of oak leaves and the inscription FOR THE CAPTURE OF BERLIN. The ribbon is red, with inset in the centre the gold and black ribbon of the old Czarist Order of St George.

BUDAPEST

This star has a hammer and sickle with a branch either side. The inscription in Russian reads FOR THE CAPTURE OF BUDAPEST. The ribbon is orange, light blue and orange of equal stripes.

VIENNA

The inscription on this star is FOR THE CAPTURE OF VIENNA, with a branch bearing twelve leaves. The ribbon is light blue, dark blue, and light blue of equal stripes.

BELGRADE

This medal is a wreath encircling the inscription FOR THE LIBERATION OF BELGRADE. The ribbon has equal stripes of green, black, and green.

PRAGUE

The lower half is in the form of a sunburst on a half wreath, and above the inscription FOR THE LIBERATION OF PRAGUE. The ribbon is mauve, blue, and mauve of equal stripes.

WARSAW

At the base of this medal is a star, rising from this a sunburst, across the centre of which is the word WARSAW on a riband; above the sunburst FOR THE LIBERATION OF WARSAW. The ribbon is blue, red, blue, and narrow yellow edges.

USSR Victory over Germany (1945)

This medal is dominated by a profile of Stalin in full dress uniform facing left. There are two mottos in Russian OUR CAUSE IS JUST and WE ARE VICTORIOUS. The ribbon is that of the Czarist Order of St George, gold with three black stripes.

Spain: The Yoke and Arrows (Yugo Y Flechas)

This is a revival of an ancient Order commemorating the defeat of the Moors by the Spanish. This badge consists of five arrows passing through a yoke and was reinstated by General Franco after he had liberated Spain from the Communist yoke of the 1930s. Although the Russian-organised International Brigade poured in fighters from all parts of the globe they proved a poor match against Franco's troops who were suitably aided by the famous German Condor Legion.

It is now a regular Order and has a sash or ribbon, depending upon the class, in black with broad red edges.

Turkey: The Order of the Medjidie

Five classes were awarded with the size of the decoration gradually decreasing according to the grade. The centre of the Badge of the first four classes is gold, and that of the fifth silver; the first three classes are worn round the neck, suspended by a crimson ribbon with green edges, whilst the other two classes suspend the Badge from the left breast by a similar ribbon. The Order is in the form of a sunburst being silver, with seven triple points or rays, between which are seven small crescents and stars of five points. On a red enamelled band in Arabic characters are the words LOYALTY – PATRIOTISM – ZEAL and the year in the Hegiran era '1268' (this being the year the Order was founded, 1852) around the cypher of the Sultan. The Order is suspended from a red enamelled crescent and star. This Order was awarded to over a thousand British Army and Navy officers for services in the Crimea, Sudan and Egypt. It is now obsolete.

Turkish War Service Cross 1914–18

A small, 1in.-diameter silver medal bearing on the obverse a Turkish trophy of arms made up of swords, cannon, flags, pikes, halberds and jewelled awards; above, in a sunburst is the Sultan's cypher. The reverse bears a Turkish inscription and the Hegiran date '1208'.

A silver bar with crossed swords below is mounted on a ribbon of red, with two thin green stripes. This medal was also awarded to German officers during World War I and can be seen on the Imperial German group of medals on page 56.

Finland: 1918 Campaign medal

A small silver-gilt medal being 1⅛in. in diameter and having a light blue ribbon with a narrow white stripe at the edges. The obverse bears the crowned head and shoulders of an angry lion, wielding a short broad-sword in an armour clad fist and arm. On the raised edges the words URHEUDESTA FÖR TAPPERHET and two roses. The reverse consists of a full wreath with SUOMEN KANSALTA, 1918 within. The medal is unnamed as issued.

Finland: Medal for the Order of the White Rose 1919

A circular steel medal 1$\frac{3}{16}$in. in diameter and bearing on the obverse a rampant lion facing left, also crowned and armed in a similar manner to the 1918 Campaign medal. Beneath its feet is an Eastern scimitar, and below this a small cartouche with S & Co. and a small head. The reverse bears a cross *patée*, with a rose and swastika superimposed; the lower two quarters have the date 1918, while in the top left quarter an armoured arm and fist wields a short broad-sword against the mailed arm and fist which wields a Turkish scimitar, in the top right quarter. The ribbon is light blue with two black stripes. There is a silver bar with the words SYD – FINLAND which can be seen illustrated on page 57 which is also sewn to the 1918 Campaign medal.

The Serbo-Turkish War medal 1912

400,000 of these medals were struck and distributed to the officers and men who took part in the Serbo-Turkish campaign.

The obverse has the Serbian Eagle, encircled by a laurel wreath with the names of the main battles engraved upon the leaves, reading downwards on the left: KUMANOVO, UESKÜB, PRILIP, ADRIANOPLE, WELLES, N. PAZAR, DEBAR, ISTIP, PRIZREN ET MEDARE; and on the right: MONASTIR, SCUTARI, OHRID, DOYRAN, SJENIZA, TETOVO, LJESCH, ELBASSAN, DURAZZO, and PRISTINA. The names are, of course, in Serbian characters.

The reverse depicts a piece of artillery captured from the Turks, with a sunburst and the date 1912 above; the Serbian inscription KOSSOVO AVENGED refers to the time when the Serbians lost their independence in 1389. This medal which bears the Swiss modeller's name, Hugounin *Frères*, is suspended from a silk ribbon, with the national colours, red, blue, and white repeated six times.

The Serbo-Bulgarian War medal for Courage

This medal was issued for valour and awarded to officers and men who had distinguished themselves in the campaigns of 1912 and 1913.

The obverse bears the bust of the Serbian national hero, Obilitch, who had been revered since 1389 and whose spirit had

German–Italian Campaign Medal in Africa (1940–3). Struck to commemorate the occupation of Egypt and the Suez (which didn't come to pass), this medal was a little premature

inspired and encouraged the Serbian people to fight for their freedom and throw off the yoke of the Turk. Around the bust of Obilitch is the Serbian inscription MILOCH OBILITCH, NATIONAL HERO, 1389. The reverse consists of the cross of chivalry, a pair of crossed swords, and a laurel wreath with the legend FOR COURAGE in the centre. The ribbon is of red silk. 27,000 of these medals were struck in bronze gilt, 4,000 in silver-plated bronze, 101 in silver, and seven in gold.

Dutch Flying Cross (Vliegerkruis)
Established by Queen Wilhelmina in 1941 to honour deeds of courage, initiative and perseverance in aircraft actually flying in time of war, either engaged with the enemy or not; this silver decoration could be bestowed upon officers and men of the Air Force, Navy or Army; and on civilians or foreigners if their action is of merit to the Netherlands.

If won more than once a 'bar' is added to the ribbon, in gold, and in Roman numerals – 'II', 'III', 'IV'. The ribbon is white with diagonal stripes of yellow.

German-Italian Campaign in Africa 1940–3

Struck to commemorate the occupation of Egypt and the Suez Canal by the Axis forces during World War II, this medal is rather unique owing to the fact they were first found aboard a sunken wreck in Bizerta harbour by the Allies in May 1943. This bronze circular medal is 1¼in. in diameter and is worn from a black, white, red, white and green striped ribbon. The obverse bears two knights in armour, personifying Germany and Italy, standing on the forelegs of a crocodile, the Allies, and forcibly clamping its jaws, the Suez Canal. On the reverse is a triumphal archway with a swastika on the right and the Italian fasces on the left. Round the rim is the legend CAMPAGNA ITALO – TEDESCA IN AFRICA and ITALIENISCH – DEUTSCHER FELDZUG IN AFRIKA. Beneath the archway is a reef knot.

As the Axis forces lost the war in Africa the medal was a little premature.

5 points of interest when purchasing medals

Enthusiasm in collecting anything is something every budding collector must possess for without it they will burn themselves out within the first few exciting months. However, there is a fine dividing line between keenness and outright fanaticism, for if you live and breath from dawn to dusk thinking of nothing else but your collection you can soon lapse over that line. This is where a tight reign of self discipline has to be applied. I am always telling folk of a collector who met this same fate: it all started with an urge to hang a pistol on the wall just to give the den a little character and atmosphere. He was given one as a present together with a book on antique firearms. After reading this from cover to cover he began to ask his friends and relatives if they had any old guns tucked away in the odd cupboard or shed. Soon he had cleared the area where he lived of anything resembling a pistol or gun and consequently had to start looking further afield for his requirements. This was all very well but he did have a nine-to-five job with only the weekends to pursue his hobby. So, the only course left open to him was to travel around after work in answer to the many advertisements which appeared in the numerous antique and gun magazines. On and on he plunged chasing after this or that phantom weapon, burning up miles upon miles of roadway just in the hope of obtaining another gun. Of course it just had to happen – after months of this kind of tearing and rushing around the countryside he ended up having a nervous breakdown, the outcome of which necessitated the sale of his entire collection to finance the three month cruise needed to restore him to health. Today he will look and talk about guns, but apart from his book he has not one piece in the house nor does he want one. All the enjoyment was driven out of his hobby by that fanatical lust to possess; it was not enough just to collect and study, he just had to chase the pot of gold sitting on the other side of the mythical fence. This may smack of sour grapes but it is so easy to become inflamed into paying way over the odds for something which may seem a bargain at the time of purchase, but given time to study and reflect turns out to be a different story.

When bidding at an auction it pays to try and inspect the medals at close quarters, searching for the name, number, regiment etc., and also the bar information. The chapter on Fakes and Forgeries should have given some of the relevant details as to what to look for in this respect. Not only will you be able to satisfy yourself that it is genuine (or not!) but also to scrutinise it for edge knocks and general wear and tear. A medal in EF condition can be reckoned to fetch double that of one in Fine condition.

Many bargains can be picked up at the odd junk-shop or jumble sale and with a little luck at antique shops, although the latter is more of a chance as most dealers tend to keep up to date with auction prices. They do trip up now and then especially on some of the little-known regimental medals which seem to them so mundane but if only they knew it are worth more than the Waterloo medal. For example, I have heard among the collecting fraternity how a medal struck to commemorate Cromwell's victory over Charles I and the Royalist cause was picked up for five shillings in a junk/antique shop way out in Norfolk. One cannot really fault the dealer, for it resembled nothing like a medal – it was more in the line of a school award. In another instance a very rare Elizabeth Armada medal changed hands among some dealers for a few pounds and later fetched four figures in a famous London sale room.

At the other end of the scale we find many shops sporting MBEs, OBEs and many other impressive looking awards marked up at very impressive prices! If these orders and medals are without any military awards they are only really worth a few pounds each because a civil servant, policeman or postman is quite likely to have been awarded one for good conduct and length of service. Not that they are to be sneered at, but from the value point of view they do become downgraded. So many novices make the mistake of purchasing a medal for its looks; rather akin to the chap purchasing his first car. Just so long as the paint is nice and shiny he doesn't even bother to check if the engine is working! Many medals that fetch high prices at auction and private sales are just ordinary, plain and simple awards. Take the Naval General Service of 1793–1840 (page 82). On comparing it with the other NGSs listed it seems little differs to make that leap from around £14 to £180. But the collector who really studies his hobby closely knows just what to look for and to snap it up whenever the opportunity arises.

Generally speaking edge knocks and erased names take off a good slice of the market value except on a rare medal. A medal that is, say, one of a dozen may never come to light again in a lifetime so one must take the plunge and purchase it, edge knocks and all. While on the subject of erased names, I feel one should explode the myth of a medal being faked if it shows signs of being erased or tampered with. Nowadays soldiers have little need to pawn their medals for beer or tobacco but the soldier of, say, 40 years ago had to do just that until his next pay day arrived. This was all very well if his posting was good and stable but with the Empire ever on the boil he was likely to be drafted overnight to the nearest port and by morning be on his way halfway across the world. Consequently, he had to find a replacement medal before his next full kit inspection, for failure to do so could lead to a Court Martial. Hence the appearance of so many medals bearing erased names. Our erring soldier having acquired the necessary award filed off the original name leaving it blank or if he was rushed, with just slight traces of lettering. I have found a number of such medals among groups and on one occasion even amidst an officer's group!

The same yardstick can be applied to edge knocks, for back in those pre-1900 days a soldier only took his uniform off when he slept. This meant that his medals were perpetually worn and over a period of years suffered somewhat from clanking against each other. Thus we find on the Khedive's Bronze Egypt 1882–91 Star

Khedive's Bronze Star 1882–91. Note the worn left-hand point on the obverse illustration. Ribbon is bright blue

Egyptian Medal 1882–9. Ribbon of white and blue. Note the pockmarks on the Queen's face and head – evidence of it having been worn next to the Khedive's Bronze Star

the right hand point of the star shows signs of wear – much more so than the other four points. Likewise on the silver Egyptian Medal the Queen's head is usually covered in tiny pock-marks; evidence of it having nestled against the Khedive's Star.

So, one must take these points into consideration when purchasing these old campaign medals and in fact I should want to see evidence of wear when buying such a group.

Many medals have their own individual stories, not for the deeds of valour that they represent but in construction or even a political *faux pas* of the day. Next time you handle a Queen's South Africa medal that has not been cleaned for some little while, take it to a window light and scrutinise very closely the area beneath Britannia's outstretched arm (reverse). Here in ghostly outline will faintly be seen the dates 1899–1900. The British Government had the medal struck with these dates thinking that the war would be over and done within the year. Not only did they have to erase the date from the QSA medal but owing to the death of the Queen in 1901 had to strike another for King Edward VII in 1902. Some of these QSA 1899–1900 medals were issued to a Volunteer Regiment of Canadian Horse who, being shipped straight back to Canada after the war received the original medal complete with dates untouched. Find one of these in your travels and you will certainly have made a killing for they are very few and far between and greatly sought after, fetching very high prices when they appear upon the market.

There are many unofficial foreign awards to British servicemen which, although earned under battle conditions, were not recognised by the War Office and consequently were not allowed to be worn whilst in uniform. Two which spring readily to mind are the 1900 Kimberley Star and the Cape Copper Company medal, 1902. These are but a few which a collector could stumble across whilst searching through a dealer's box of odds and ends. The most important thing is to study all the sale catalogues that come your way, likewise any military data, for only by handling and studying these are you likely to recognise that rare medal if and when you come across it.

Something which the novice collector with limited means could collect are the very petite miniature medals, reproductions of the

Africa General Service Medal with Somaliland 1902–4 Bar. Note that the AGSM is never seen without a bar

genuine awards but only worn by officers and senior NCOs in uniform evening dress or in mufti. These miniatures can be purchased very cheaply and are to be found dating back to around 1820 although the first illustrated evidence of their existence is in photographs taken after the Crimea. They are struck for most of the world's fighting forces, and those of the Eastern hemisphere have great beauty and delicate workmanship.

1 Nazi Wound Badge (silver) **2** Group as worn, Iron Cross 2nd Class, Medal of 1 Oct 1938, Memel Medal **3** Iron Cross 1st Class **4** War Merit Medal **5** Gallipoli Star 1915 **6** Russian Front Medal 1941–2 **7** Iron Cross 2nd Class 1914 **8** War Merit Cross 2nd Class with Swords **9** Imperial German Service Medal 1914–18

6 medals of germany

Here we open up a field of collecting which covers nearly 135 years of Germanic history. Not only do we touch the many Prussian States – now swallowed up and forgotten – but the fascinating period from 1933 to 1945, when the whole of Germany became a united and powerful fighting machine under the rule of Adolf Hitler. Whatever the world may think of Hitler as a man it must acknowledge his capacity for organisation – be it the WHW (Winter Relief Work), or the well oiled machinery of the Waffen SS.

All had medals and orders whatever the organisation and many have taken years to identify owing to the complete destruction of anything Nazi after World War II. Many were awarded to volunteer divisions formed in occupied countries such as Holland, Norway, Finland, Czechoslovakia and Croatia. At the end of the war many members of these divisions were either incarcerated in Russian forced labour camps, or those who did manage to escape the slaughter on the Eastern Front took refuge in the many Displaced Persons' Camps scattered around Europe. Their medals and insignia were discarded in their headlong flight, exchanged or bartered for a few cigarettes or pieces of bread. It has only been during the past few years that certain students and collectors of NSDAP militaria have traced the many hitherto unknown medals and badges of these organisations.

Although prices of medals in general have risen a great deal over the past year or two the price of anything connected with

Nazi Germany has risen twofold, so much so that the market is being flooded with fakes and re-strikes.

The chapter on fakes and forgeries will prove of some help to the novice, but only experience by viewing and handling the genuine articles will give the collector that little bit of know-how.

Hanover medal

Among the first medals struck for German soldiers was the Hanover medal. It was issued by command of the Prince Regent of Great Britain, and awarded to the surviving soldiers and relatives of those men who had fallen at Waterloo. The medal is $1\frac{5}{16}$ in. in diameter and bears on the obverse the laureated head of the Prince Regent facing to the right, with draped truncation, and surrounded by the inscription GEORG · PRINZ · REGENT 1815. On the reverse in the centre is WATERLOO JUN. XVIII, flanked by laurel wreaths, with a trophy of arms above, and encircled by the inscription HANOVERISCHER TAPFERKEIT. The medal was suspended from a large steel ring and clip by means of a crimson and blue-edged ribbon along the same lines as the British Waterloo.

Brunswick medal

This medal was also ordered by the Prince Regent (as guardian of the minor Princes of Brunswick), and issued to the soldiers of Brunswick who were present at the actions on 16, 17, and 18 June 1815. This medal was struck in 1818 from captured French cannon.

On the obverse it bears the head of Duke Frederick Wilhelm of Brunswick, who was killed at the battle of Quatre Bras, and the inscription in German lettering reads FRIEDRICH WILHELM HERZOG.

On the reverse is the date 1815, encircled by a wreath of oak and laurel, and the inscription in German arranged round and divided by rosettes, BRAUNSCHWEIG SEINEN KRIEGERN. QUATREBAS UND WATERLOO. (Brunswick to her Warriors. Quatre Bras and Waterloo). The medal is $1\frac{3}{8}$ in. in diameter, was suspended from a steel ring and clip by a $1\frac{1}{2}$ in. yellow ribbon, with broad stripes near the edge. The officers' medals were gilt, with the names engraved on the edge.

Hanover Jubilee medal

This bronze medal was presented by the inhabitants of Hanover on the anniversary of the battle of Waterloo to the survivors of the Hanoverian Brigade. The arms of Hanover are on the obverse encircled with the inscription STADT HANOVER DEN SIEGERN VON WATERLOO 18 JUNI 1815, and on the reverse, within a laurel wreath, ZVR 50 JÄHRIGEN JUBELFEIERAM JUNI 1865.

Saxe-Gotha-Altenburg medal

Struck in 1816 on the orders of the Duke Emilius Leopold Augustus, this bronze medal was awarded to the members of the Foreign Legion of the Duchy of Saxe-Gotha-Altenburg who had taken part in the campaigns of 1814–15.

The obverse bears the Altenburg rose and an ornamental border, while the reverse has the ducal crown and the legend IM KAMPFE FUER DAS RECHT (In the struggle for right), and around the edge, HERZOGTH GOTHA-VND-ALTENBVRG MDCCCXIV: MDCCCXV. The medal has a ball-shaped loop and ring for suspension from a 1in. wide, dark-green ribbon with a border of black flecked with gold braid.

Prussian König Grätz Cross 1866

A war between the Prussians and the Austrians which lasted just seven weeks and ended in complete victory for the Prussians, showed the world at large how far superior the breech-loading needle-fire rifle was against the old-fashioned muzzle-loader used by the Austrians. At the battle of Sadowa, the Austrians lost 20,000 men killed or wounded, with as many prisoners. The Prussian losses were a mere 10,000.

The Cross bears in the centre the Royal Cypher W.R., surrounded by the legend PREUSSEN SIEGREICHEM HEERE (To Prussia's victorious army); on the upper arm of the Cross is the Prussian crown, on the left arm WAR UNS SEI, on the right arm GOTT MIT IHM, and on the lower arm DIE EHRE. On the reverse is the crowned Prussian eagle, sitting on a cannon; on the upper arm is KÖNIG-GRATZ, on the right JULI, on the left DENZ, and on the lower arm, 1866. The ribbon is of black corded silk, 1in. wide, with narrow stripes of white and orange at the edges.

German Franco-Prussian medal 1870–1

At the end of the Franco-Prussian War the German Emperor issued medals of bronze or iron to combatants and non-combatants, who rendered service during the campaign: the reverse will explain whether it was awarded to one or the other. The combatants' medal bears on the obverse a large 'W', being the initial of Wilhelm, surmounted by the Prussian crown, and beneath, DEM SIEGREICHEM HEERE (To the victorious army), encircled by GOTT WAR MIT UNS, IHM SEI DIE EHRE (God was with us, to Him the honour).

On the reverse, surrounded by a wreath of laurel, 1870 · 1871. The steel medal has the wreath of oak, but on both medals the wreath overlays an Iron Cross with a sunburst issuant between the arms.

On the edge is sometimes found engraved AUS EROBERTEM GESCHUETZ (from captured guns). The medal awarded to non-combatants bears the inscription FÜR PFLICHTTREUE IM KRIEGE (for faithful service in war); there is no inscription on the edge. The ribbon is 1in. wide, of ribbed silk, with a red stripe down the centre, and black and white stripes with black edging.

1813 Prussian Iron Cross

This Cross, which laid the foundation for Iron Crosses of both world wars, was instituted by King Frederick William III on 10 March 1813 to reward those, either military or civil, who distinguished themselves in the war of that time. It was divided into three classes, the Grand Cross, which was double the size of the Knight's Cross, and worn round the neck, was awarded exclusively for the gain of a decisive battle, the capture of an important position, or the brave defence of a fortified position. The first class recipients would also wear upon the left breast, instead of a Star, a similar Cross or Badge. Regulations governing the award of this Cross allowed all ranks to be eligible.

For those worn by the military the ribbon was black with two white stripes near the edge; and by civilians with a white ribbon with black edges. At the close of hostilities the Order was suspended but was reintroduced on 19 July 1870 for the Franco-Prussian War.

The decoration is a cast-iron Cross, in the form of a cross *patée*, with silver borders and mountings. There are three classes, both for military and civilians. On the obverse, in the centre, within a silver milled border, are three oak leaves; above, FW surmounted by the Prussian crown, below, the date 1813. The Cross awarded for the 1870 war differs on the reverse by having in the centre, also within a silver milled border the initial W, with a crown above, and below, 1870. Recipients of this award who were awarded another during the 1914–18 War received a bar with a miniature cross superimposed, but this was only worn on the ribbon of a 2nd Class.

Just how the Iron Cross came about makes interesting reading. It appears that back in the Napoleonic Wars, the women of Germany gave up their jewellery to help pay for arms, equipment, etc. and instead had pieces of jewellery executed in iron. These delicate pieces were real works of art and, today, can be viewed among the other treasures in the Victoria and Albert Museum, London. As a mark of respect to the women of Germany the medal ordered by the King was to be the Iron Cross – a medal which has become one of the world's most popular and sought-after awards.

·

1815 Prussian Oval Iron medal

This oval, iron medal bears on the obverse King Frederick William's initials surmounted by the Prussian crown and beneath in German, FÜR PFLICHITTREUE IM KREIGE (For faithful services in war); encircling this is the legend GOTT WAR MIT UNS, IHM SEY DIE EHRE (God was with us, to Him the honour). The reverse has a cross *patée* with sunbursts between the arms and in the centre 1815. The ribbon is of white watered-silk with black and yellow stripes. It was awarded to non-combatants.

Prussian Campaign medals for 1813–15

Awarded by King Frederick William III to all those who took part in the campaigns of 1813–15, this bronze medal has on the obverse the initials FW surmounted by a crown; below in German, PREUSSENS TAPFERN KRIEGERN (To Prussia's brave warriors), surrounded by the legend, with a border, GOTT WAR MIT UNS, IHM SEY

DIE EHRE (God was with us, to Him the honour). On the reverse, within an oak and laurel wreath, upon a cross *patée* with sunbursts, is 1815 – the campaign date. Engraved around the edge is AUS EROBERTEM GESCHÜTZ (from captured guns). The ribbon is yellow, with black and white stripes.

Austrian Cross 1814–15

This is rather an interesting award as the Cross itself is enamelled green, likewise the laurel wreath which connects the arms of the Cross. On the obverse, across the centre arms, is PRINCEPS ET PATRIA, on the upper arm GRATI, and on the lower arm FRANC IMP AVG. The reverse bears across the centre arms LIBERTATE ASSERTA, on the lower arm MDCCCIII MDCCCIV; and on the upper EUROPAE. The corded ribbon is yellow with broad black edges.

Hessian medal 1814–15

A bronze medal $1\frac{1}{8}$in. in diameter, bearing on the obverse in German text, K.W.II REINEN TAPFERN HESSEN, 1821, surmounted by a crown, and encircled by a wreath of oak leaves. On the reverse is a cross *patée*, the arms resting upon a wreath of laurel. The dates 1814 1815 are in the centre. Two spears are arranged between the arms. Over the top arm, and resting upon a circle enclosing a light wreath, is a helmet, encircled by a motto GOTT BRACH DES FEINDES MACHT UND HESSEN WARD BEFREIT. On the edge is engraved AUS EROBERTEM GESCHÜTZ (from captured guns). The ribbon is dark-blue with wide red edges.

German South West Africa 1904–6

Once again two medals were struck, one in bronze for combatants, and one in steel for non-combatants.

On the reverse we find the richly helmeted head of Germania, surrounded by the inscription, SUDEWEST AFRIKA, 1904–6, and on the reverse the Imperial crown with ribbons surmounting the Gothic initial W.II, which is above crossed swords. Encircling this is the inscription DEN SIEGREICHEN STREITERN.

The ribbon is white with a series of red horizontal lines down the centre, leaving a clear white margin, which is edged with a black border. A gilt bar KALAHARI 1908 is attached to the ribbon, but as it is only sewn on it is very likely to get lost.

German Pour le Mérite

Originally a Prussian Order founded by Prince Frederick, later Frederick I of Prussia, c. 1667 as the Order of Generosity, it was later to become the Order of Merit in 1740. In 1810 it was awarded for military merit against an enemy in the field of battle; and then later in the 1840s it had a civil class added, a different badge for science and art.

During the Franco-Prussian War and World War I the Order was the highest award for individual gallantry in action, and among those to receive it was that World War I German air-ace, Hermann Göring. This award, which fell into disuse after the 1918 War, was worn around the neck from a black ribbon with stripes of white interwoven with silver braid. It took the form of a Maltese Cross in blue enamel, edged with gold, and with four golden eagles between the arms. The upper arm has the letter 'F' in gold surmounted by a crown, and 'Pour - le - Mé - rite' on the other arms.

A higher class of the Order does exist, but with a spray of three golden oak leaves worn on the suspension ring, and an extra silver central stripe on the ribbon.

The few medals listed of the Prussian States are but a small selection, for to list them all would fill a complete book.

Hohenzollern House Order with Swords 1851

This is a very impressive cross patée with rounded arms, enamelled in white and black. The obverse bears the Prussian eagle in the centre, enamelled in black and gold upon a white background. On a blue riband encircling the centre is the inscription VOM FELS ZUM MEER and beneath, in green and gold, tied branches of laurel. Superimposed upon a green enamelled wreath which encircles the complete cross, are a pair of gold swords. The large Imperial crown which is pinned to the medal top acts as a suspender for the black and white ribbon.

The reverse is similar in design except for the white enamelled centre which has a crowned cypher in gold. On the blue riband, above the laurel branch, DEN 18 IANUAR. 1851.

Hamburg 1914 War Service Cross

A cross *patée* in silver with the obverse enamelled dark-red upon a sunburst base, the centre bears a triple-turreted castle in silver. The reverse is plain silver with the inscription in the centre F R VERDIENST IM KRIEGE 1914. The ribbon is white with dark-red stripes on the edges.

Bavaria, Order of Military Merit

Once again a beautifully executed piece of work in the form of a Maltese Cross in silver with flames of silver issuant from the four corners. The centre of the obverse is black enamel bearing a superimposed crowned 'L' in gold. Around this centre is a white and gold enamelled garter with the word MERENTI also in gold. Attached to the suspender ring is a crossed pair of silver swords. On the reverse, upon a black enamelled centre, is a gold, crowned rampant lion. The white and gold garter bears the date 1866 also in gold. The ribbon is white, with two narrow blue stripes and thinner stripes of black at the edges.

Mecklenburg Schwerin 1914 War Service Cross

Struck in gilded bronze this cross *patée* resembles the popular Iron Cross except that it is constructed in one piece. On the obverse upper arm, in German is FÜR, and across the left and right arms

An important group of Imperial German medals worn in Prussian Style.

They are, from left to right: German Iron Cross 1914 2nd Class; Hohenzollern House Order with Swords; Hamburg 1914 War Service Cross; Bavaria, Order of Military Merit; Mecklenburg Schwerin 1914 War Service Cross; Oldenburg, Frederick 1914 War Service Cross; Lubeck War Service Cross; Weimar Republic 1914–18 War Service Cross; Prussia, Officers' 25 years' Service Cross; Finland, 1918 Campaign Medal; Finland, Medal for the Order of the White Rose; Turkey, War Service Cross. This group is valued at £50

AUSZEICHNUNG IM, and on the lower one KRIEGE. The reverse has the Imperial Crown on the upper arm, FF in the centre, and 1914 on the lower arm. The ribbon is pale blue with a stripe of yellow and red on the edges.

Oldenburg, Frederick 1914 War Service Cross
Struck in black enamelled iron this sombre award is a cross *patée* with a full wreath between the arms. The obverse bears on the top arm the Imperial Crown, on the centre FA, and on the lower arm the date 1914. The reverse is devoid of an inscription and is plain. A bar, with VOR DEM FEINDE was issued which pinned on the dark-blue, red edged ribbon.

Lübeck War Service Cross
Yet another medal in the form of a cross *patée* with dark-red enamel upon a silver sunburst base. The centre bears a double-headed eagle in black and red enamel with a red and white shield on the breast.

The reverse is of frosted silver with an inscription in the centre FÜR VERDIENST IM KRIEGE 1914. The ribbon is white with broad red edges.

Weimar Republic 1914–18 War Cross
A rather poor example of war medal is the Wiemar 1914–18 War

Iron Cross 2nd Class 1939 (obverse and reverse)

Service Cross. Struck in bronzed steel it takes the form of a cross *patée* with crossed swords between the arms, and the centre formed from a full laurel wreath. The dates 1914–18 are within the wreath on the obverse. The reverse is completely plain except for the maker's mark. It is suspended from a ribbon with a dark-red centre stripe, then black, white and black stripes either side.

Prussia, Officers' 25 years' Service Cross

This medal is also in the now familiar cross *patée* style and is struck in frosted gilt ormolu with the centre containing a crowned royal cypher, and III, on the obverse. The reverse has just XXV in the centre showing the length of service the officer had completed. The ribbon is dark blue.

The Iron Cross

So much has been written about the Iron Cross over the last few years that little remains to be said except for some military and technical data which hitherto has been overlooked.

As I have already mentioned this Cross was instituted by Frederick Wilhelm, King of Prussia, for the War of Liberation against Napoleon in 1813.

Although regulations decreed that the Iron Cross 2nd Class would be worn from the buttonhole with the crowned FR, three oak leaves, and 1813 on the obverse side it was in fact worn with the reverse showing. This idea became so popular that a decree was issued in 1938 making this practice official. It was also a condition that a 1st Class could not be awarded unless the 2nd

Class had also been awarded. A grand total of over 5,000,000 2nd Class Iron Crosses, and 218,000 1st Class were awarded during World War I.

The next change came in 1939 when Hitler renewed the Iron Cross, but now it was upgraded to an Order. This Cross bears on the obverse a swastika in the centre and 1939 on the lower arm. The reverse has just a plain black area with 1813 on the lower arm. The 1st Class has a plain silver back with either a vertical brooch pin or screw-back fitting which allows it to be worn on the left breast pocket. For World War II the awards of 2nd Class Crosses are well over 6,000,000, and around 750,000 of the 1st Class.

The ribbon has also seen a series of changes since it was first instituted. For 1813, 1870-1, and 1914-18 it was black with two white stripes near the edges; in 1939 the centre has a wide red stripe with a white and black stripe either side.

So, at the time of World War II the Order was now graded into the following groups:

The Grand Cross (64mm × 64mm)

The Knight's Cross with golden oak leaves and swords & brilliants (48mm × 48mm)

The Knight's Cross with silver oak leaves, and swords & brilliants

The Knight's Cross with oak leaves, and swords

The Knight's Cross with oak leaves

The Knight's Cross

1st Class Iron Cross (44mm × 44mm)

2nd Class Iron Cross (44mm × 44mm)

The Grand Cross and the Knight's Crosses were worn at the throat, while the 1st Class was pinned on the left breast without a ribbon, and the 2nd Class was worn together with other awards on a bar above the left breast pocket.

Recipients of the 1914 Iron Cross who also won a 1939 type were allowed to wear their original award but with an eagle and swastika bar mounted on the ribbon of the 2nd Class, or clipped to the tunic above the 1st Class.

Among the many thousands who won the Iron Cross was Adolf Hitler who won his 1st Class in 1917, and one of the youngest holders of the Knight's Cross was Günther Nowack, just sixteen years old, a member of the Hitler Youth and seconded into the ranks of the Volkssturm towards the end of the 1939–45 War. Alone he disabled nine Russian tanks by placing linked grenades into vulnerable positions as they lumbered by his fox-hole. After the final surrender he was taken prisoner and shipped to a Russian Prisoner of War camp where, it was learned later, he was to die.

An English double-agent, Eddie Chapman, who spied for the highest bidder, also rates among those who are allowed to wear the Iron Cross.

Before starting on the medals of the NSDAP I have listed the different organisations that one is likely to find while hunting for German awards. Many of these decorations are in the form of a badge, for the dividing line between medals and badges is so thin that they do have a tendency to overlap each other.

organisations of the Third German Reich, 1933–45

NFS	National Socialist Women's Organisation
NSRDS	National Socialist State League of German Sisters (Nurses)
NSDF	National Socialist German Women Workers
RDF	State League of German Families
NSRL	National Socialist State League for Physical Training
DAF	German Labour Front
NSKOV	National Socialist Organisation for Relief of War Victims
WHW	Winter Relief Work
SS	Elite Guard
WAFFEN SS	Elite Guard Forces (Combat Units)
SD	Security Service
SA	Storm Troops (Brown Shirts)
NSV	National Socialist People's Charities
NSKK	National Socialist Vehicle Corps
NSFK	National Socialist Flying Corps

HJ	Hitler Youth (Ages from 14–18)
DJ	German Youth (Ages from 10–14)
BDM	German Girls' League
RAD	State Labour Service
OT	Organisation Dr Fritz Todt
TENO	Emergency Technical Assistance
NSDA	National Socialist German Doctors' League
NSBDT	National Socialist League of German Technicans
NSL	National Socialist Teachers' League
NSADA	National Socialist League of Older German Students
DAV	National Union for German Elements Abroad
DRK	German Red Cross
NSBO	National Socialist Farmers' Organisation

The 'Blood Order' was originally ordered for issue to those of the Party before 1933, but was then awarded for outstanding deeds up to 1945

One of the first founders of the SS was Julius Schreck, here shown in full SS uniform complete with the Gold Party Badge. This was in fact originally issued to those with a number below 100,000, but was awarded for outstanding deeds up to 1945

Deutsches Kreuz (German Cross)

Instituted by Adolf Hitler during World War II it was the highest German Order that could be won. There were three classes, gold with brilliants, gold, and silver; the gold being awarded for courage in the face of the enemy, the silver for 'leadership of men'. It takes the form of an eight-pointed sunburst Order, with a large swastika set within a wreath, and 1941 at the base. It has no ribbon and is worn on the right breast by a pin-brooch fitting. These were also made in braid, and silk, to be sewn onto the number two or three tunic.

The Blood Order

This medal was granted to all those who took part in the bloody 'putsch' in Munich in 1923. The obverse bears a proud eagle settling upon a wreath of oak which has 9 NOV. within, and MÜNCHEN 1923–1933 inscribed to the right. On the reverse is the Feldherrnhalle in Munich, with a swastika emitting rays above. The upper circumference has the inscription UND IHR HABT DOCH GESIEGT (And yet you have conquered). The ribbon is red, black and white. It was worn threaded through the right breast pocket buttonhole and was usually seen worn by leading Party members on the November Party Day.

Gold Party badge

This coveted award was worn in uniform if it had been awarded to members of the NSDAP before 30 January 1933. It consists of a circular badge with a black swastika upon a white background in the centre, around this a red circle with the inscription NATIONAL SOZIALIST D.A.P. in white. Around the whole a wreath of gold laurel leaves which denotes the wearer was a member of the party before 1933. It was worn just below the left breast pocket flap.

Wound badges

Worn on the left breast like the badge of an Order, this award had three classes; gold for five or more wounds; silver for three or four; and black for one or two.

The Naval award was oval with crossed swords superimposed on an anchor, the whole surrounded by an oval of anchor chain.

The Army badge is likewise oval with crossed swords sur-mounted by a steel helmet bearing a swastika, the whole sur-rounded by a laurel wreath. The reverse is plain except for a maker's mark. They had no ribbon.

On 20 July 1944 three further awards were instituted. The three classes are gun-blue and silver, silver, gold. According to existing records only 11 recipients received this solid silver (800 fine) badge which bore on the obverse the usual steel helmet, swastika, crossed swords and laurel wreath. It differs from the original by having beneath the helmet 20 JULI 1944, and a facsimile of Adolf Hitler's signature. Fakes do exist but they are rather poorly finished and without the L/12 800 on the reverse.

Battle Shields

For those who took an active part in the conquest of certain countries a Battle Shield was awarded. These were struck in thin bronzed brass which was sewn or clipped onto the left sleeve. They were: KRIM.1941–1942; KUBAN.1943; CHOLM.1942; NARVIK.1940; DEMJANSK.1942; and LAPPLAND.

Russian Front medal

A rather sombre, but befitting medal to all who fought with such vigour on the Eastern front.

The obverse bears the hunched eagle upon a squared swastika, above, as part of the suspender ring, a steel helmet with a stick grenade beneath.

The background is concave with a gun-blue finish. The reverse is convex and bears the inscription WINTERSCHLACHT IM OSTEN 1941/42, and beneath a sword and laurel branch. The ribbon is red, white, with a thin centre stripe of black.

Sudeten medal

A circular medal of gilt brass, it bears on the obverse two allegorical male figures moving to the right. The larger (Germany) holds the Party banner in his left hand, while assisting the smaller figure (Sudetenlander), to mount a rostrum. On the reverse the inscription 1 OKTOBER 1938. EIN VOLK ϟ EIN REICH ϟ EIN FÜHRER ϟ. This medal was awarded for the occupation of the

'Sudetenland'. The ribbon is black, with a centre stripe of red, and thin white edges.

Memel medal
This is a circular medal bearing the same design as on the Sudeten medal. The reverse bears the inscription ZUR ERINNERUNG within a wreath of oak. The ribbon is green, white, red, white.

Protectorate medal
This is the same as the Sudetenland medal, but was issued with a bar, officially known as 'Clasp to the medal of Bohemia and Moravia in March and April, 1939'.

The West Wall medal
A bronze oval medal awarded to those who assisted in building the 'Siegfried Line', it was suspended from a khaki-coloured ribbon with narrow white edges, and worn from the second buttonhole of the uniform tunic. On the obverse there is an eagle and swastika, crossed sword and spade, and a bunker. The reverse bears the inscription FÜR ARBEIT ZUM SCHUTZE DEUTSCHLAND (For work in defence of Germany).

The War Merit Cross, 1st Class
Instituted in 1939 this silver Cross is only one step beneath the Iron Cross. It takes the form of a Maltese Cross with a swastika within a wreath in the centre, on the obverse.

The reverse also has the oak wreath centre with 1939. It was issued without a ribbon and with a pin back, and could be awarded with or without 'swords' which indicated whether it was won in action or not.

The War Merit Cross, 2nd Class
Similar in design to the 1st Class except that this award is struck in bronze and is suspended from a ribbon with black, red, and white stripes. It was also awarded with or without 'swords'.

Spanish Campaign Honour Cross
Similar in design to the War Merit Cross 1st Class, it was also

The German Merchant Navy Blockade Runner's award, as issued with miniature. Complete in original case it is now worth £5

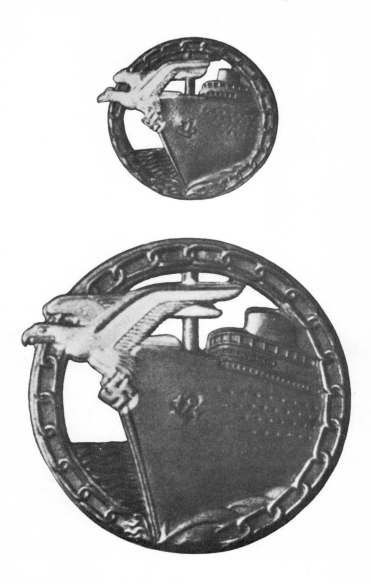

issued with or without 'swords', and was worn on the breast like the badge of an Order. It had no ribbon; and had four classes – gold with brilliants, gold, silver, and bronze which were awarded according to the rank and service of the recipient. Four eagles span the arms on those awarded to the Condor Legion of the Luftwaffe who assisted in the Spanish Civil War of 1936.

Knight's Cross of the War Merit Cross
A little larger than the other War Merit Crosses, this medal was struck in solid silver and worn from the neck suspended by a ribbon. It was awarded only on the authority of Hitler, who also presented it.

War Merit medal
A circular medal of bronze it bears on the obverse the design of the Merit Cross. The reverse carries the inscription FÜR KRIEGSVERDI- ENST. 1939. The ribbon is similar to the Merit Cross except for a thin red stripe in the centre.

Spanish Volunteers in Russia medal 1941–2
A circular medal bearing on the obverse a German steel helmet with two shields surmounted upon a broadsword. The left hand shield has an eagle and swastika while the right has a yoke and five arrows of Spain. Beneath is a squared swastika and laurel branch. On the reverse is the inscription DIVISION ESPANOLA DE VOLUNTARIOS EN PUSIA. Beneath this a branch of laurel and oak above an Iron Cross.

This medal which was issued to members of the Blue Division was worn from a white ribbon with one edge of red, yellow, red, and the other of black, white, red, white, black.

Blockade Runner's medal
A circular medal 2in. in diameter, struck in steel and finished in a matt battleship-grey colour. There is no ribbon and it is fitted as an Order with a brooch-pin mount. The obverse depicts the bows of a liner moving left and breaking through the links of a chain which form a border. A large silver gilt eagle which acts as the ship's figure-head is also shown breaking the chain barrier. The

reverse bears the maker's name. This medal was awarded to members of the German Merchant Navy who supplied vital spares and fuel to the fighting forces of the Third Reich. Issued in a velvet lined case there is also a miniature to wear for evening mess duty.

Guerilla Warfare Award

This was instituted in 1944 and awarded to the many branches of the Third Reich who were fighting against Communist partisans on the Balkan Front. The obverse depicts five serpents coiled around a short broad-sword which bears the sign of the 'wheeled' swastika. Surrounding the whole is a wreath of oak with a skull and crossbones at the base. There is no ribbon, as it is worn like an Order by a brooch-pin fitting.

England's most coveted award, the Victoria Cross, and, fetching
anything from £1,000 upwards, one of the most sought after medals

7 the victoria cross

The chances of adding a Victoria Cross to one's collection are very remote indeed because not only are they a very coveted award and therefore few and far between, but their prices when sold are usually well outside the wallet of the average collector. For a World War I VC one could expect to pay from £750 upwards; for a World War II VC from £1,000. If the medal is part of a group then of course the price rises accordingly. Fakes do exist and potential buyers should always seek professional advice before purchasing.

Instituted by Queen Victoria in 1856 to cover the Crimean War period, it was awarded to any officer or man who performed an outstanding deed of gallantry in the face of the enemy. It consists of a bronze cross *patée*, $1\frac{1}{2}$in. across with raised edges. The obverse has a lion statant gardant upon the Royal Crown, while below the crown on a semi-circular scroll are the words FOR VALOUR. The reverse also has a raised edge with the date of the action engraved in the centre. Name, rank and ship or regiment is engraved on the back of the suspender clasp, which is ornamented on the front with laurel leaves. One outstanding feature of this clasp is the large V which together with a plain ring links it to the medal. In the first instance the $1\frac{1}{2}$in. ribbon was blue for the Navy and red for the Army but a Royal Warrant of 22 May 1920 decreed that in future the ribbon would be crimson for all the Services.

When the ribbon only is worn a small replica of the Cross is mounted in the centre. Bars are awarded for subsequent acts of gallantry which are also in the form of a small bronze replica of the Cross.

For the Crimean War alone 111 Victoria Crosses were awarded, 62 of these being presented by Queen Victoria in Hyde Park on 26 June 1857, one year after the close of the war.

Holders of the Cross were entitled to a pension of £10 a year with an extra £5 for each bar. However, in 1898 the pension could be increased to £50 where the recipients were proved to be in financial difficulties. In July 1959 the pension was raised by the then Prime Minister, Harold Macmillan, to £100 a year tax free to all VCs regardless of rank and wealth.

As this is a much coveted award and one that holds a most honourable distinction it was ordained that 'if any recipient was convicted of cowardice, treason, felony or any other infamous conduct, he will have his pension stopped and his name erased from the register'. Since that first investiture in 1857 and through the different wars that have ensued over the past 114 years a total of 1,351 Crosses (including 3 bars) have been awarded and only eight recipients have fallen by the wayside to earn the dishonour of forfeiture, the last being in 1908.

Although this award is open to all ranks, male or female, to date no member of the fair sex has won a VC.

Before 1902 if a Victoria Cross was won by a man who was killed in action it was the practice to enter his name upon the official Gazette, but his Cross was not awarded to the next of kin. However, King Edward in 1902 issued an order to the effect that posthumously earned Victoria Crosses were to be bestowed upon relatives.

After the 1914–18 War the Victoria Cross was awarded to the American Unknown Warrior, but strangely enough not to the British Unknown Warrior interred in Westminster Abbey.

There are only three instances of men winning the Victoria Cross twice, the first being Surgeon-Captain A. Martin-Leake, South African Constabulary, who won it in 1902 during the South African War, plus a bar for gallantry in France between 29 October and 8 November 1914. The second, Captain G. Chavasse, RAMC attached to the 1/10th Battalion Liverpool Regiment, won his VC on 9 August 1916 at Guillemont, France, and won a posthumous bar at Wieltje, Belgium, between 31 July 1917 and 2 August 1917. In World War II 2nd Lieutenant C. H. Upham, 20th Battalion New Zealand Military Forces, won his VC at Maleme, Crete, between 22 and 30 May 1941, and his bar on 14 July 1942 at El Ruweisat Ridge.

The story behind each and every Victoria Cross awarded could fill a book* so I have selected just a few from the time the Cross was first instituted, through the Indian Mutiny and the Zulu War, Boer War, World Wars I and II and on to Korea and Vietnam.

If one was to try and describe the calibre of man that constitutes a VC winner it could only be summed up in one word – tenacity! For in nearly every case cited the man or boy concerned displayed courage and complete disregard for his own safety. Many of the recipients laid down their lives in that one act of valour – others gambled with death and lived to tell the tale.

It would only be fitting to start with the first-ever VC which was won by 20-year-old Mate Charles Davis Lucas aboard HMS *Hecla*, during the heavy bombardment of the fortress of Bomarsund on 21 June 1854. At the time cannon were charged from the muzzle and the balls and shells heated red-hot before loading. The shells were hollow and either filled with molten lead, pitch or hundreds of tiny steel balls, which burst upon impact scattering a deadly load around the deck. The type of shell that landed alongside Charles Lucas and his gun crew was one filled with explosives and a short time fuse set to explode a few seconds after impact. Lucas, without any afore-thought, scooped the spluttering missile up and tossed it over the ship's side where it exploded with a terrific roar. He was promoted to Lieutenant on the spot and was decorated by Queen Victoria at Hyde Park on 26 June 1857.

No account of the Crimean War would be complete without that famous Charge of the Light Brigade and of the terrible massacre that ensued. The leading line of the Light Brigade consisted of the 13th Light Dragoons and the 17th Lancers. The second line consisted of the 4th Light Dragoons, 11th Hussars and the 8th Hussars. The cannon-fire from the left, and to the right and at the head of the valley, as well as the hordes of Russian

* *The Story of the Victoria Cross 1856–64* by Sir John Smyth, published by Frederick Muller.

riflemen tore through them as they thundered down that 'Valley of Death'. But they made it, cutting down the Russian gunners with their razor-sharp sabres – they were so sharp in fact they could sever a man in two with one well-aimed blow. The Victoria Crosses for Balaclava were as follows: Troop Sergeant-Major John Berryman, 17th Lancers; Lieutenant Alexander Robert Dunn, 11th Hussars; Sergeant John Farrell, 17th Lancers; Sergeant-Major John Grieve, 2nd Dragoons (Scots Greys); Sergeant-Major Charles Wooden, 17th Lancers; Private Samuel Parkes, 4th Hussars; Sergeant Joseph Malone, 13th Light Dragoons; Surgeon James Mouat, 6th Dragoons; and Sergeant Henry Ramage, 2nd Dragoons (Scots Greys).

At the battle of Inkerman, 5 November 1854, a total of 19 Victoria Crosses were awarded in a battle where men fought with anything they could lay their hands on. Men, who after receiving terrible wounds struggled on to do battle with the enemy. Such a man was Brevet-Major Charles Lumley of the 97th Regiment. Being one of the first to enter the Redan at Sebastopol on 8 September 1855, he fought off three Russian gunners killing two before being knocked unconscious by a large rock. Regaining his senses he drew his sword and led his men to the attack only to receive a musket ball in the mouth. But even this did not put him out of action permanently for he was present at that first investiture in Hyde Park to receive his VC from Queen Victoria!

The last VC survivor of the Crimea was Surgeon-Major Henry T. Sylvester, who died at the age of eighty-eight on 13 March 1920. Serving with the 23rd Regiment in the assault on the Redan on 8 September 1855, he won his VC by venturing out beyond the front line trench to dress the wounds of a dying fellow-officer while under heavy enemy bombardment.

Age doesn't seem to be a barrier when faced with a difficult and dangerous task, for we find eighteen examples of Victoria Crosses being won by lads under twenty, while the oldest known man ever to receive the VC was Lieutenant William Raynor who was a member of the Bengal Veteran Establishment. He was thought to be sixty-nine at the time of his award which was earned at the Dehli Magazine, during the Indian Mutiny, on 11 May 1857.

Only on three occasions has the VC been won in Great Britain;

This unique photograph was taken the morning after Lieutenant William Leefe Robinson had shot down the German airship L33, thus becoming the first man to win the VC in Great Britain, 3 September 1916

An artist's impression of Lieutenant N. J. Coghill and Lieutenant
T. Melvill who died in the vain attempt while trying to save the
Colours at the massacre of Isandhlwana 1879

it was won by Lieutenant William Leefe Robinson, of the Worcestershire Regiment and the Royal Flying Corps, who on 3 September 1916 'attacked an enemy airship under circumstances of great difficulty and danger and sent it crashing to the ground as a flaming wreck'. This was the first time that a pilot had shot down a German airship (the L33) on English soil.

Acting Leading Seaman Jack Foreman Mantle, RN was awarded a posthumous VC earned inside Portland Harbour. On 4 July 1940, Mantle stayed by his AA gun aboard the merchant cruiser HMS *Foylebank* after being wounded many times. Thirdly and lastly, there was the case of Flight-Lieutenant James Brindley Nicholson, 249 Squadron, RAF, who on 16 August 1940, while engaged in a dog-fight above Southampton was shot-up, his plane set alight and himself wounded, but despite his wounds he engaged another German fighter-plane which he managed to shoot down. Although badly burned he lived to receive his Cross.

One of the most enthralling periods in British military history was that of the Zulu War where primitive savages armed only with a long throwing spear, a stabbing assegai and a hide-covered shield completely wiped out over 1,300 European and native troops at Isandhlwana on 22 January 1879. It would be wrong to assume that these Zulus were undisciplined or untrained in the art of warfare, for their King Cetywayo had formed an army of 45,000 men organised into corps and regiments who would charge through a hail of bullets to thrust their well-balanced and deadly assegais into the young Redcoats. As the British Army was still experimenting with the single-shot breech-loading Martini Henry rifle which had the nasty habit of getting the thin brass cartridge jammed in the breech-housing, thus wasting valuable shooting time while the soldier rammed it out, it was little wonder the 20,000 Zulus massacred those 1,329 soldiers at Isandhlwana.

Three Victoria Crosses were won at Isandhlwana: two to officers, Lieutenant N. J. Coghill, 1st Battalion 24th Regiment, and Lieutenant T. Melvill, also of the 1st Battalion 24th Regiment, and to a Private S. Wassall, 80th Regiment. The two young subalterns died while attempting to ride off with the Queen's Regimental Colours in the vain hope of saving it from falling into enemy hands. Private Wassall earned his VC for saving a comrade from drowning in the Buffalo River while under heavy fire of the muzzle-loading muskets that the Zulus had now acquired.

If the massacre at Isandhlwana is remembered as a British military failure then the battle at Rorke's Drift will be remembered as one of human endurance and gallantry in which eleven Victoria Crosses were won. The garrison consisted of only eight officers and 131 men, mainly from the 24th Regiment. Thirty-five of these were sick and in the hospital, which was built of stone and roofed with dried grass. The enemy, the Undi Corps, consisted of 3,500 well-trained warriors who having tasted blood earlier that day at Isandhlwana plunged into the attack expecting to accomplish the same swift results once again. How wrong they were!

Although the battle lasted twelve long hours in which the British lost 15 killed and a dozen wounded, the enemy lost 350 killed with untold numbers wounded.

The eleven VC winners at Rorke's Drift on 22 and 23 January 1879 were Corporal W. Allen, 2nd Battalion 24th Regiment; Lieutenant G. Bromhead, 2nd Battalion 24th Regiment; Private F. Hitch, 2nd Battalion 24th Regiment; Private H. Hook, 2nd Battalion 24th Regiment; Private R. Jones, 2nd Battalion 24th Regiment; Private W. Jones, 2nd Battalion 24th Regiment; Lieutenant J. R. Chard, RE, Acting Assistant Commissary; J. Dalton, Commissariat and Transport Dept; Surgeon-Major J. Reynolds, Army Medical Dept; Corporal F. Schiess, Natal Native Contingent; and Private J. Williams, 2nd Battalion 24th Regiment.

During the Indian Mutiny (1857–9) we find the first VC awarded in 1858 was won by Lieutenant Frederick Sleigh Roberts, of the Bengal Artillery, who distinguished himself on a number of occasions and in later life was to become that famous British commander, Lord Roberts. His only son, the Hon. Frederick H. S. Roberts, King's Royal Rifle Corps, was killed in action while trying to rescue a battery of besieged field-guns during the South African war on 12 December 1899. For this he was awarded the Victoria Cross, and the gun that he had died trying to save was later given to his father by the War Office.

By the time the 1914–18 conflict was well under way warfare as such had ceased to be so distinctive and sporting as it had in previous wars. This was the period of massive artillery bombardments and with men fighting and dying for a piece of barren ground some 100 yards away! Between 2 August 1914 and 30 April 1920 633 Victoria Crosses were awarded, 186 of these being posthumous awards. Among the latter is the name of Boy (1st Class) John Travers Cornwell who faced death with cool courage and steadfastness. Aged sixteen-and-a-half years he was mortally wounded while serving his gun at the battle of Jutland, 31 May 1916.

The Second World War was a much more mobile war with machines playing a far more active part in the conflict. The VCs won during this period were well earned with the recipients having to cope with damaged tanks, aircraft, submarines and fast ships, besides the usual tribulations encountered in the course of battle.

The first VC of this war was won by Lieutenant Commander G. B. Roope, RN, serving aboard the 1,345-ton destroyer HMS *Glowworm* in Norway on 8 April 1940, while engaged in action against the 10,000-ton German cruiser *Hipper*. Although the battle was completely one-sided the *Glowworm* caused considerable damage to the German ship when, battered, blasted and burning from stem to stern, she rammed the *Hipper* and then capsized and sank. Only one officer and 30 men out of a complement of 149 lived to tell the tale.

One of the 132 Victoria Crosses to be won during the last year of the war was that posthumously awarded to a Naik Fazal Din in Burma on 3 May 1945. Naik Fazal Din, commanding a section of the 7th Battalion 10th Baluch Regiment, took on a party of six Japanese. During the struggle he received a blow from a Japanese officer's Samurai sword which pierced his body through. As the officer withdrew his cherished blade Fazal Din managed to wrest it from his hands and killed him; he then went on to kill another Japanese with this sword before collapsing and dying at his platoon HQ.

During the Korean War four VCs were won with two posthumous awards going to Major K. Muir, 1st Battalion Argyll and Sutherland Highlanders, on 23 September 1950 at the battle of Hill 282, and Lieutenant P. Curtis, 1st Battalion Duke of Cornwall's Light Infantry, at the battle of Imjin River on 22–23 April 1951.

Whenever Korea is mentioned in military circles one can never forget the fighting spirit of the Gloucestershire Regiment, 'The Glorious Gloucesters'. For just as their forefathers had won the right to wear two cap badges – one on the front and a similar smaller one at the back, to commemorate a back-to-back stand during the battle of Alexandria, Egypt, in 1801 – they fought on until all ammunition was exhausted and their positions overrun. Lieutenant-Colonel J. P. Carne, of the 1st Battalion The Gloucestershire Regiment was captured along with the remnants of his battalion and was to suffer a long solitary confinement. His VC was won in the action at the Imjin River, 22–23 April 1951.

The last Korean War Victoria Cross winner was that veritable giant of a man, Private William Speakman, 1st Battalion Black Watch (attached to the 1st Battalion King's Own Scottish Borderers). Bill Speakman decided to drive off the enemy who had overrun his section's position. Calling upon a party of six other comrades to keep him supplied with hand grenades he engaged in a series of grenade charges causing the enemy heavy casualties.

The following Victoria Crosses have been awarded since the Korean War:

London Gazette

21148768 L/Cpl RAMBAHADUR LIMBU   22 April 1966
10th Princess Mary's Own Gurkha Rifles, Sarawak

29890 WO II K. A. WHEATLEY
(Posthumous)   15 December 1966
Australian Army Training Team, Vietnam

4100 Major P. J. BADCOE (Posthumous)   13 October 1967
Royal Australian Infantry Corps, Vietnam

217622 WO II SIMPSON   29 August 1969
Royal Australian Infantry Corps, Vietnam

12222 WO II K. PAYNE   19 September 1969
Royal Australian Infantry Corps, Vietnam

8 medals of the united kingdom

So many medals have the right to be included in this chapter I find it very hard to wield the axe and cut their numbers down to fit within the limited space. The ones I have listed are not necessarily superior to those left out, but in my humble opinion seem to be a little more interesting.

Naval General Service medal 1793–1840

Although this medal was awarded to men serving from 1793 it was not issued until 1848. The obverse bears the young head of Queen Victoria and the date 1848. The reverse shows a seated figure of Britannia upon the back of a sea-horse, with a laurel branch in her left hand and a trident in her right. The suspension clasp is plain and in silver as is the medal. The ribbon is a wide section of white edged with navy blue.

The men who could lay claim to this medal served aboard the 'Wooden Walls of Old England' in the struggle against the French, and saw service under Lord Nelson at the Nile and Trafalgar. One point of interest being that a medal was awarded to a baby – one 'Baby' Daniel Tremendous McKenzie who was born just before the battle of 1 June 1794 aboard HMS *Tremendous*. It was the custom to let certain seamen take their wives to sea with them. It is a known fact they helped to service the guns when called upon to do so. One woman was known to have claimed, and actually been awarded this medal after doing battle at Trafalgar on 21 October 1805. However, it was later rescinded by the Admiralty and struck off the Rolls.

All told there are 230 different engagement bars bearing either the name of the ship involved, the name of the action, or the words BOAT SERVICE. In some cases medals will be found named to Army personnel who served aboard His Majesty's ships instead of the usual contingent of Royal Marines.

The Waterloo medal 1815
This being the first British official war medal it is found with either the official steel ring or unofficial bar suspender. Struck in silver it carries on the obverse the effigy of the Prince Regent, with the words GEORGE P. REGENT. The reverse bears the winged figure of Victory seated on a plinth bearing the word WATERLOO. Round the top circumference is the name WELLINGTON, and at the bottom the date JUNE 18TH, 1815. The ribbon is 1½in. (sometimes 2in. wide), and is dark-crimson with blue edges.

Every schoolboy knows the history of the battle of Waterloo so I shall not bore the reader with mundane political history. However, as this book is concerned primarily with the history of war medals I shall set out some of the deeds which earned the participants the right to wear the Waterloo medal.

The French numbered 90,000 and the allied forces 74,400. The day opened with the crashing fire of over 200 pieces of artillery –

Naval General Service Medal 1793–1840 with Syria Bar
(obverse and reverse)

a fitting overture for such a field of battle. At Hougomont the Coldstreams and Scots Guards held on to their positions even after a full day of bloody warfare. In all some 3,825 British soldiers died.

At the famous charge of the Union Brigade, Lord Anglesey, observing that the French lancers and cuirassiers were preparing to make a flank attack upon the British infantry, wheeled the Royals, Royal North British Dragoons (Scots Greys), and Inniskillings into line, charged and overwhelmed the French cavalry. It was in this charge that Sergeant Ewart of the Scots Greys captured the Eagle of the 45th Regiment; the Eagle of the 105th Regiment was captured by Captain Clarke of the Royal Dragoons thus securing the right for these regiments to wear the Eagle badge.

The loss in individual regiments was terrible. Four hundred men of the 27th were mowed down in a square without firing a single shot. (Their medals in EF condition are very rare and could command their own price.) The 92nd reduced to some 200 men made a daring attack upon a column of 2,000 French, and with the aid of the Scots Greys routed them. Time and time again the cream of the French army assisted by a murderous artillery bombardment drove deep into the squared ranks of the British. The King's Own German Legion was completely annihilated by

The Military General Service Medal 1793–1814 with Talavera Bar

the French, while seventy-seven squadrons made a desperate effort to pierce those stubborn but thinning squares of British infantry.

In vain did the ten battalions of the Imperial Guard, led by Marshal Ney, push their way up the slopes between Hougomont and La Haye Sainte, for the Foot Guards – with the 52nd, 71st and 92nd Regiments – offered such a murderous reception the Guards turned and fled. No wonder Napoleon ejaculated, '*A présent c'est fini – sauvons nous!*' for Wellington was ordering the whole line to advance; the weary, hungry, and even wounded soldiers rushed forward and forced the retreat which, as the British leader with the 42nd and 95th threw himself on Ney's flank, and the allied cavalry charged the enemy's columns, became an utter rout.

The Old Guard, that elite body of men on whom Napoleon had placed so much, made a grand but ineffectual stand against the British and Prussian cavalry who, with the smell of victory in their nostrils, ploughed through them and turned the two square miles of Belgian territory into a field of carnage. Little wonder that Wellington, when recrossing the battlefield and viewing the

The British Waterloo Medal of 1815 (obverse and reverse)
Note the original iron ring and clip

50,000 dead or wounded men and horses, declined his supper that evening!

The following regiments were present at Waterloo:

2 squadrons 1st and 2nd Life Guards; 2 squadrons Royal Horse Guards (Blues); 1st Dragoon Guards; 1st Royals*; 2nd Royal North British Dragoons* (Scots Greys); 6th Inniskilling Dragoons*; 12th, 13th, 16th Queen's and 23rd Light Dragoons; 7th, 10th Royal; 15th King's; 18th Hussars; 2nd and 3rd Battalions 1st Foot Guards (Grenadiers); 2nd Battalion 2nd Foot Guards (Coldstreams); 3rd Battalion 3rd Foot Guards (Scots Guards); 3rd Battalion 1st Royal Scots; 1st Battalion 4th; 3rd Battalion 14th; 1st Battalion 23rd Royal Welsh Fusiliers; 1st Battalion 27th Inniskilling*; 1st Battalion 28th (Gloucesters); 2nd Battalion 30th; 1st Battalion 32nd; 33rd; 1st Battalion 40th; 1st Battalion 42nd Black Watch*; 2nd Battalion 44th; 51st; 1st Battalion 52nd; 2nd Battalion 69th; 1st Battalion 71st Highland Light Infantry; 2nd Battalion 73rd Perthshires (2nd Battalion Black Watch); 1st Battalion 79th Cameron Highlanders; 1st Battalion 92nd Gordon Highlanders; 1st, 2nd, and Prov. Battalions 95th; 8 Troops Royal Horse Artillery; 6 Brigades Royal Artillery; Corps of Royal Artillery Drivers; Royal Foot Artillery; Royal Engineers; Royal Sappers and Miners; Royal Waggon Train; Field Train Department of the Ordnance; Royal Staff Corps; Commissariat Dept; Ordnance Medical Department, and the following units of the King's German Legion: 1st and 2nd Light Dragoons; 1st, 2nd, and 3rd Hussars; 1st, 2nd, 3rd, 4th, 5th, and 8th Line Battalions, and 1st and 2nd Light Battalions; the total present being about 2,308 officers and 42,120 non-commissioned officers and men.

The medals marked * are very rare and always command a high price whenever they appear upon the market.

The Crimea 1854–6

Struck in silver, the obverse of this medal bears the young head of Queen Victoria and the wording, VICTORIA REGINA with the date 1854 beneath the head. The reverse shows a rather striking figure of a Roman warrior armed with a shield and gladius whilst a winged figure of Victory crowns his head with a wreath of laurels. The word CRIMEA is inscribed vertically on the left. The medal was worn from a pale blue ribbon with yellow edges. The bars for this medal are in the form of oak leaves with the name of each engagement in the centre. Bars issued are INKERMANN, ALMA, BALAKLAVA, SEBASTOPOL and AZOFF, the latter being issued to the Navy for operations in the Sea of Azoff.

In October 1853 the Czar of all the Russias declared war against the Sultan of Turkey – to defend her, Great Britain and France rushed troops to Varna, a Bulgarian port in the Black Sea. At the end of February 1854 Queen Victoria bade farewell to the Guards at Buckingham Palace, and these with other regiments sailed out for far distant shores to a wild country which was to cost the lives of 21,815, either by direct cause of battle or disease, and 11,876 wounded. How ironic it all was to think that disease alone accounted for 16,041, and battle just 4,774!

This was the time when the old muzzle-loading rifle and musket had reached its peak of performance: in the hands of a good soldier it could kill at four hundred paces and with the newly accepted Minie bullet,* could blast the arm or leg off a man if so hit in that area. Add to this the wicked looking triangle bayonet measuring a good eighteen inches long, and you can see how the British earned their title as being among Europe's best soldiers.

During the bloody battle of The Alma the Welsh Fusiliers, who were among the first to land at the Crimea, lost their colonel and eight officers, and the Light Division lost 47 officers and 850 men. The Division was composed of the 7th, 19th, 23rd, 33rd, 77th and the 88th. The Russians had 5,000 placed *hors de combat* including 45 officers.

The regiments present at The Alma were the Grenadier, Coldstream and Scots Guards; 1st, 4th, 7th, 19th, 20th, 21st, 23rd, 28th, 30th, 33rd, 38th, 41st, 42nd, 44th; two companies of the 46th, 47th, 49th, 50th, 55th, 63rd, 68th, 77th, 79th, 88th, 93rd, 95th, Foot; 4th and 13th Light Dragoons; 8th and 11th Hussars and the 17th Lancers. On this occasion the cavalry were never called into action. As Lord Raglan remarked, 'I prefer to keep my cavalry in a band-box.'

When one recalls the Crimean War one is apt to forget the

---

* A lead bullet weighing 1oz, having a hollow base sometimes filled with an iron or hard-wood wedge with two rings at the waist to grip the rifling.

drawn-out siege of Sebastopol and think only in terms of The Charge at Balaclava. Such is the terrible glory of war; only the swift and exciting deeds seem to lodge in the memory but of those who died in the year-long siege (28 September 1854–11 September 1855) little or nothing is heard. The conditions under which men had to live were appalling for, while high-ranking officers lived the life of country gentlemen complete with picnic hampers, servants and the whole family on hand, the men and junior officers died like flies in pools of mud and water. Between November 1854 and February 1855 there were 9,000 deaths in hospital, and by the end of February there were no less than 13,600 officers and men in hospital. Hospitals as such were the crudest form of shelter with worn-out bell tents, mud floors and a meagre ration of meat and weevily biscuits to comfort the wounded. It was in such conditions as these that the 'Lady with the Lamp', Florence Nightingale, tried her best to succour and relieve the pain of the dying and wounded with what little medicines made available to her. This was to be the turning point in British military history; it was only after Miss Nightingale had petitioned for better medical conditions that the Medical Staff Corps was formed in 1855; later to become the Army Hospital Corps in 1857, and finally in 1918 the RAMC.

The battle of Balaclava opened on 25 October 1854, the anniversary of Agincourt. The Russian force, numbering 22,000 infantry and 3,400 cavalry, with 78 guns, advanced across the Woronzoff Road to attack the front of the position at Balaclava, and to confront them Lord Raglan took down the First and Fourth Divisions to the plain, which General Canrobert reinforced with the First Division of French infantry and the Chasseurs d'Afrique.

It was during this battle that the 93rd Highlanders, with 100 invalids in support, stood their ground and drove off 400 of the enemy's cavalry thus becoming known as that famous 'thin red line'.

By now the Russians had become rattled to the point of throwing in some 3,000 horsemen, against the British Heavy Brigade, being 900 sabres strong. With Brigadier-General Scarlett leading about 300 Scots Greys and Inniskillings into the fray the

"All that was left of them"

J. T. Herbert
James Mustard
James Olley
George Gibson
John Box

1854 1912

VIIIth Hussars
XIth Hussars
IVth (Queens Own) Light Dragoons
XIII Light Dragoons
XVIIth Lancers

Matthew Holland
John Parkin

J. A. Kilvert
P. Briers
Henry Wilsden

Edwin Hughes
John Whitehead
William S. J. Fulton
W. H. Penning

SURVIVORS OF THE CHARGE OF THE LIGHT BRIGADE.

Survivors of the Charge of the Light Brigade as they were in the year 1912. Now only ghosts but whose deeds live on through their medals whole Russian force was put to rout by sheer steel and courage.

Lord Raglan, seeing that the withdrawal of the Russians should be taken advantage of to regain the heights, and fearing that the enemy might attempt to remove the guns from the captured Turkish redoubts, gave orders for the Light Cavalry to be moved forward. Captain Nolan misconstrued this order, and instead, indicated to Lord Lucan that the heavy battery of guns a mile away, supported by masses of cavalry and infantry, with other batteries on either flank, was to be charged. Orders being orders the Earl of Cardigan rode with his Light Brigade of 621 men into the 'valley of death'. Encircled by fire they charged down the valley, dashed through the guns, sabred the gunners where they stood, and cut their way through a brigade of Russian cavalry and a company of infantry. Four squadrons of Lancers were hurled at them, but they met the charge well, whilst the Russian artillerymen, recovering from their shock, turned their guns upon both British and Russians alike! If it hadn't been for a diversion created by The Greys and Inniskillings together with the Chasseurs d'Afrique it is doubtful whether a single man would have survived to tell the tale.

Four hundred and twenty-six of the brigade were placed *hors de combat*, 13 officers and 162 men were killed or taken prisoner; 27 officers and 224 men were wounded. In all there struggled back to camp, in scattered groups, a remnant of 195 mounted men.

The regiments engaged at Balaclava were the Heavy Brigade, comprising the 1st, 2nd, and 6th Dragoons; 4th and 5th Dragoon Guards; the Light Brigade, consisting of the 13th Light Dragoons and 17th Lancers in the first line, 4th Light Dragoons and 8th and 11th Hussars in the second line, and the 93rd Highlanders. Men of the Rifle Brigades, and the artillery and various line regiments, including the 4th, 19th, 21st, 30th, 33rd, 44th, 47th, 50th, 53rd, 68th, and 77th were all present and received the medal with the bar for Balaclava.

The Crimea medal was issued unnamed, as was its naval counterpart, the Baltic; however, some recipients of the former had their name and regiments engraved privately. Others were officially named later, with the same stamps as were used for the Army General Service and early Kaffir War medals, in square Roman capitals.

The Sudan Medal for 1896-7. Awarded to all those troops who took part in the reconquest of the Sudan. Ribbon is black, yellow, with a thin centre stripe

The India General Service Medal. Instituted in 1854, it was awarded up to 1895

The bars should read upwards from the medal as follows: ALMA, BALAKLAVA, INKERMANN, SEBASTOPOL, but as a number of the medals were issued without the bars being fixed, many are found in the wrong order and in some cases minus the odd bar; care should be taken to verify the record of the person named on the medal.

Turkish Crimea medal
This medal, also struck in silver, was awarded by the Turkish Government to British, French and Sardinian troops who served in the Crimea on her behalf. It was suspended by a bright red ribbon with green edges threaded through a small silver ring. As these medals carried in the exergue either CRIMEA 1855, LA CRIMEA 1855, or CRIMEE 1855, it has often puzzled the novice collector to find in a British group perhaps the French or Sardinian award. The answer to this is that the ship bringing the medals to England foundered and British troops received one of the other two medals instead. Another guide is to study the trophy of flags on the reverse; next to the Turkish flag is either the British, French or Sardinian colours depending upon the nationality of the recipient.

French Crimea medal
The Emperor awarded crosses of the Legion of Honour to officers and men for conspicuous service during the war, and the Médaille Militaire to about 500 non-commissioned officers and men who had distinguished themselves. The medal is silver, the eagle and centre being gilt, and the band surrounding the head of Louis Napoleon enamelled, likewise that on the reverse. The centre bears the inscription VALEUR ET DISCIPLINE.

Turkish General Service medal
This medal was awarded by the Turkish Government in 1855 to the officers and 30 men serving aboard a British gunboat, and to a Colonel and 16 men of the Royal Engineers, for services rendered on the Danube in 1854. On the reverse is an elliptical star of 12 points, with a smaller one of 6 in the centre; beneath is a scroll bearing in Persian characters the inscription *'Mischani Iftikar'* (Medal for Glory). Struck in gold for officers and silver for the

Punjab Medal 1848–9 with two of the three bars awarded with
this medal. The other bar that could be won was 'Mooltan'

men, it was suspended from a silver scroll bar by the same ribbon
as the Turkish Crimea medal.

First Indian General Service medal 1854

Sanctioned by Queen Victoria, on the recommendation of Lord
Dalhousie, the then Governor-General of India, this silver medal
bears the young head of Victoria and the legend VICTORIA REGINA.
The reverse has a figure of Victory crowning with a laurel wreath
a seated warrior in a classic pose, holding in his right hand a
Roman sword, and in his left the scabbard. The ribbon, $1\frac{3}{4}$in.
wide, is dark crimson with two dark blue stripes. Rank, name, and
regiment or ship is engraved in Roman capitals for PEGU, PERSIA,
NORTH-WEST FRONTIER, UMBEYLA, BHOOTAN, but for PERAK and the
rest of the bars, except JOWAKI, lightly engraved Roman capitals
were used. Altogether there were 23 bars given for different 'little
wars' stretching over a period of forty-one years.

India Medal 1895
Waziristan 1901–2 Bar

The first bar, that for PEGU, was awarded to those who participated in the Burmese War of 1852–3. Regiments entitled to this medal and bar were the 18th, 51st, and 80th; Artillery; Sappers and Miners; 1st Bengal Fusiliers; 1st Madras Fusiliers; 5th Madras Native Infantry; and the Naval Brigade from 13 of Her Majesty's ships. Many men lost their lives in the swamp and jungles, while disease alone claimed the lives of 365 officers and men of the 18th Royal Irish.

The India Medal 1895

This medal was to be known as 'The India Medal 1895' but the bars are the same in design as those on the former India medal. The obverse has the legend VICTORIA REGINA ET IMPERATRIX together with an effigy of Queen Victoria. The reverse shows a British and an Indian soldier each supporting the Standard. The word INDIA and the date 1895 are at the side.

The suspender is in the form of an ornamental scroll while the ribbon is crimson with two light green stripes. As this medal was instituted after the Defence and Relief of Chitral the first bar is for the DEFENCE OF CHITRAL 1895, and was awarded to the following: Sir George Robertson, KC, SI, and 6 officers; Surgeon-Captain H. F. Whitchurch, 90 of the 14th Sikhs, 300 of the 16th Punjabis, and 4th Kashmir Rifles, assisted by about 40 servants. One interesting point is that this medal is somewhat thicker than the '54, and weighs $1\frac{1}{4}$oz. instead of 1oz.

Indian General Service medal 1903
This medal is identical in every detail to that of the 1895 on the reverse, except for the removal of the date. It bears on the obverse the same bust of King Edward VII as appears on the South Africa medal, 1902. The suspender is the same, likewise the ribbon. On this new issue the bar for WAZIRISTAN 1901–2 was given to those who saw action in the Mahsud Waziri blockade between November 1901 and November 1902. To those already in possession of the 1895 medal the bar only was issued. Bronze medals were issued to authorised camp followers. Only three English soldiers received the medal – men of the Cheshires who were employed as signallers. The troops engaged were: 1st, 3rd, and 4th Sikhs; 2nd, 4th, 5th, and 22nd Punjabis; 1st, 3rd, and 5th Punjab Cavalry; Sappers and Miners.

Indian General Service medal 1908
One of the last medals to be issued during the reign of Edward the Peacemaker, this award replaced the IGSM of 1903. The obverse bears the uniformed bust of King Edward VII, encircled with the legend EDWARDVS VII KAISAR-I-HIND. On the reverse there is a fort on a hill-top with mountains as a backing, while in the foreground encircled inside branches of oak and laurel is the word INDIA. The bar bears NORTH-WEST FRONTIER 1908. The ribbon is dark blue with green edging.

The regiments engaged in the campaign were: the Gordon and Seaforth Highlanders; Royal Irish Rifles and Royal Munster Fusiliers; the Northumberland Fusiliers and Warwickshire Regiment; 10th Hussars; 71st Company RGA; 6 guns of the 18th and

80th Batteries RFA; 62nd and 75th Batteries RFA; 2nd, 3rd, 8th, 21st, 22nd, 23rd, and 28th Mountain Batteries, and Nos. 1 and 7 British Field Hospital; 1st, 4th, 5th, and 6th Goorkas; 19th, 20th, 21st, 22nd, 25th, 28th, 29th, 30th, and 33rd Punjabees; 15th, 23rd, 34th, 45th, 53rd, 54th, 55th, 57th, and 59th Sikhs; 40th Pathans; Queen's Own Corps of Guides Infantry; Cavalry of the Queen's Own Guides; 21st Cavalry; 19th and 37th Lancers; Sappers and Miners, and 5 Native Field Hospitals.

The Ashanti medal 1896

This very distinctive medal struck after the troubles with King Prempeh in which Prince Henry of Battenburg died from fever, was believed to have been designed by Princess Henry. It consists of a St Andrew's Cross bisecting the corners of a four-pointed star, over which is a circular centre containing the Imperial crown surrounded by a plain band inscribed ASHANTI above, and 1896 below. On the back, in raised letters, is the inscription: FROM THE QUEEN. Suspended from a yellow ribbon, with broad black stripes near the edge, by means of a ring, this bronze medal was issued unnamed. However, the Colonel of the Yorkshires did have the name of each of his men and the regiment engraved upon their stars.

The Abyssinian medal 1867–8

Awarded to all Her Majesty's British and Indian forces, military and naval, who were engaged in the operations in Abyssinia between 4 October 1867, and 19 April 1868, this rather unique medal is quite outstanding in design. Being considerably smaller than others issued at this period it has on the obverse the bust of Queen Victoria, crowned and veiled, facing left, encircled by a star of nine points with the letters of the word ABYSSINIA between the angles. On the reverse, within a beaded circle surrounded by a laurel wreath, tied at the base, the recipient's name, rank, and ship or regiment are engraved in the centre. This is also an outstanding feature as nearly all other military awards are engraved around the edge. It is suspended from a silver swivel ring attached to a crown soldered to the top of the medal (which is $1\frac{1}{4}$in. in diameter) by means of a red, with broad white borders, $1\frac{1}{2}$in. wide ribbon.

This war was directed against Theodore 'The Negus' or Emperor of Abyssinia who had taken upon himself to incarcerate members of the British Consul together with other European residents in his territory. The outcome of this action was to bring a force of about 4,000 British and 8,000 Indian troops under the leadership of Sir Robert Napier into the area with great rapidity and across a most difficult and mountainous country.

Used for the very first time in actual warfare the new breech-loading Snider rifle cut the enemy to pieces with each rifleman having fired some ninety rounds of ammunition within the hour. Then the guns and rockets from the Naval brigade opened fire upon Magdala, the capital. Theodore tried to sue for peace by releasing the prisoners together with a present of sheep and cattle, but with richer prizes at stake the British stormed the fortress on Easter Monday, 13 April 1867. The fortress seized, it was discovered that Theodore had committed suicide after being deserted by his troops. With the capital looted then destroyed the British withdrew and left Africa by the end of June 1868.

The following troops were engaged: 4th, 26th, 33rd, 45th; Royal Artillery and Engineers; 3rd Dragoon Guards, and the following Indian regiments: 1st, 2nd, 3rd, 10th, 18th, 21st, 25th, and 27th Bombay Infantry; Bombay and Madras Sappers and Miners; 3rd Bombay Cavalry; 10th and 12th Bengal Cavalry; Scinde Horse, and a Naval Brigade consisting of 83 men, armed with twelve 12-pounder rocket tubes. The men from Her Majesty's Ships *Octavia, Dryad, Spiteful,* and *Satellite* took part as the rocketeers.

The China medal 1842

This medal was granted in January 1843 to commemorate 'the signal successes of Her Majesty's Naval and Military forces', both Native and European, upon the coast and in the interior of the Chinese Empire. The obverse bears the diademed head of Queen Victoria facing to the left, with the legend VICTORIA REGINA on either side (this, by the way, being the first medal issued bearing the Queen's head). The reverse consists of a trophy of military and naval arms, with an oval shield bearing the Royal Arms in the centre, against a background of a palm tree, and above ARMIS EXPOSCERE PACEM, with CHINA and the date 1842 beneath.

The suspension clasp is of german-silver and is straight and plain. It takes a red with broad yellow edge ribbon 1⅖in. wide. Naming of this medal was impressed upon the edge in bold Roman capitals.

This war was brought about by dubious British business operations which entailed the trading of opium.

Adding insult to injury to Her Majesty's Government by destroying £2,000,000 worth of opium, the Chinese Government soon brought the wrath of the British about their heads in the form of an invading force under the leadership of Brigadier-General Burrell in June 1840.

Abyssinian Medal 1867–8 (obverse and reverse)

Although the Chinese heavily outnumbered the British and Indian army their firearms were of the matchlock variety, a weapon which last saw service in European armies during the first half of the seventeenth century, some two hundred years beforehand. Therefore they succumbed to the advance of the British and Indian infantry suffering heavy losses all along the line of fortifications. Several overtures for a peaceful settlement were attempted but the Emperor had no intention of being told what to do in his own domain and issued a mandate for the total extermination of the British.

The British in turn marched upon, and conquered one by one the following Chinese garrisons: the Island of Amoy; Chusan; Chinghai and the city of Ningpo, then Tsekee; Segon and Chapoo at the mouth of the Shanghai River; in June they took Woosung and Poonshau, and the city of Shangee, then on to Chin-Kiang which fell after a terrible struggle on 21 July 1842. By the time Lieutenant-Colonel Sir Hugh Gough had led his army to the ancient walls of Nankin, on 9 August 1842, the Chinese were ready to agree to a peace treaty with the ports of Amoy, Ningpo, Foo-choo-foo, and Shanghai opened to British traders, and Hong Kong ceded to Great Britain.

The army of some 3,000 men was composed of the 18th Royal Irish, 26th Cameronians, 49th, 55th, 98th, 37th Madras Infantry, Royal and Indian Artillery, and a Naval Brigade taken from the following ships: HMS *Druid, Melville, Wellesly, Blenheim, Blonde, Conway, Volage, Larne, Alligator, Pylades, Modeste, Cruiser, Nimrod, Columbine, Algerine,* and *Rattlesnake.* The ships and crews of the Honourable East India Company also played their part together with a iron-clad steamer *Nemesis*, which played havoc with the Chinese junks. The *Herald, Atalanta, Enterprise, Calliope, Queen, Madagascar,* and *Samarang* were all part of the HEIC contingent. The following ships saw service with the fleet from time to time: HMS *Driver, Starling, Plover, Vixen, Cornwallis, Vindictive, Hazard, Endymion, North Star, Cambrian, Clio, Wanderer, Pelican, Hebe, Serpent, Royalist, Wolverine, Harlequin,* plus the hospital ship *Minden.* Further HEIC steamers to assist were: *Auckland, Akbar, Memnon, Hooghley, Pluto, Medusa, Proserpine, Sesostris,* and *Phlegethon.*

The China medal 1857–60

This medal granted in February 1861 is identical in design to the 1842 China medal, except the date 1842 has been left out and the suspension clasp is ornamental as opposed to the plain german-silver clasp of the former. The bars issued to this medal were: CHINA 1842 to those serving in the first war (very rare indeed), CANTON 1857, TAKU FORTS 1858, TAKU FORTS 1860, PEKIN 1860, and FATSHAN 1857 awarded to marines and seamen only. First issued with a ribbon of five stripes, blue, yellow, red, white, and green, it was later replaced by a crimson ribbon with yellow edges. Naming of the medal is impressed on the edge in Roman capitals, although most of those issued to the navy were unnamed with the exception of those to the marines and members of the Indian Navy.

One of the rare issues from this war is a two-bar TAKU FORTS 1860 and PEKIN 1860 to the 1st Dragoon Guards, there only being two squadrons of this regiment present. The only five-bar medal issued was to a gunner in the Royal Marine Artillery, and has the bars for FATSHAN 1857, CANTON 1857, TAKU FORTS 1858, TAKU FORTS 1860, and PEKIN 1860.

The second Chinese War flared up in Fatshan Creek during 1857. It was more of a naval battle between 11 gunboats of the British and 80 junks armed with 800 guns of the Chinese force. Later an allied army of British and French sailed right up to the walls of Pehtang Forts in the Gulf Pecheli, and then marched on to do battle at Sin-Ho.

The war finally came to an end with the city of Pekin being taken by the allies on 13 October 1860. As Lord Elgin had given his word that the city would be spared if it were to capitulate, he only ordered that the Summer Palace, consisting of some 30 buildings stretching over six miles, should be put to the torch, but only after the contents of the palace had been removed to a safe and proper place! The Palace took two days to burn down. The works of art in ivory, gold, and exotic jewellery had never before been seen by Europeans let alone handled by them. An order by Sir Hope Grant for all British troops to hand in their loot for a grand public auction met with some little success, as it is known that the share for just a private soldier was around £4 each! But this must have been the tip of the golden iceberg compared to the huge fortunes carried off by French and British officers. Many had not the faintest notion of the great wealth they held in their hands – take the French officer who parted with a string of beautiful pearls, each the size of a sparrow's egg, for £3,000!

The following regiments saw action: 1st, 2nd, 1st Battalion 3rd, 31st, 44th, 59th, 60th, 67th, 99th; Royal Artillery; Sappers and Miners, and two squadrons 1st Dragoon Guards; 11th and 19th Bengal Lancers; 20th and 23rd Bengal Cavalry.

The Afghanistan medal 1878–80

The Afghanistan medal which was granted on 19 March 1881 has on the obverse a crowned head of Queen Victoria surrounded by the legend VICTORIA REGINA ET IMPERATRIX. On the reverse the scene is dominated by a group of marching soldiers, native cavalry, and mounted officers together with an elephant carrying a gun upon its back; the background being a fortress-capped mountain. In the exergue is impressed the date 1878–9–80 while above in raised letters AFGHANISTAN. The ribbon for this medal, $1\frac{1}{4}$in. wide, is green with broad, crimson edges, the suspender being straight. Six bars were issued for the following battles: ALI MUSJID, PEIWAR KOTAL, CHARASIA, AHMED KHEL, KABUL, and KANDAHAR.

This war was the outcome of the British being shown the front door by Shere Ali of Afghanistan, who, having accepted military and monetary assistance from the British in 1869, now refused to accept a British Resident at Cabul and instead placed Afghanistan under the guardianship of Russia. Britain unleashed the Dogs of War and dispatched a military mission to Cabul which only reached Ali Musyid before being forcibly stopped. War was declared on 21 November 1878 and was to be the backcloth for many daring escapades on both sides with Major-General (later Field-Marshal Lord) Frederick Roberts, VC, making an indelible entry in the history books of the future.

Troops engaged at Ali Musjid on 21 November 1878, were the 17th, 51st; 4th Battalion 60th; 81st; four Batteries of Artillery; 10th Hussars, and the following native regiments: 4th Goorkas;

1st Sikhs; 6th, 14th, 20th, 27th, and 45th Bengal Infantry; 11th Bengal Lancers and the Bengal Sappers and Miners.

At Peiwar Kotal the following were involved: the 8th and 72nd, a squadron of the 10th Hussars, and the following native regiments: 2nd and 5th Punjab Infantry; 5th Goorkas; 23rd and 29th Bengal Infantry, and 12th Bengal Cavalry.

The battle of Charasia saw the following regiments in action: 92nd, 72nd, and 67th; a battery of the Royal Horse Artillery; one battery Royal Field Artillery; two Mountain Batteries, and 9th Lancers. Native regiments as follows: 5th Goorkas; 5th Punjab Infantry; 5th Punjab Cavalry; 12th Bengal Cavalry; 14th Bengal Lancers; Bengal Sappers and Miners.

One of the most exacting battles, Ahmed Khel, blooded the 59th; 2nd 60th Rifles, and a battery of artillery; 2nd Sikh; 15th, 19th, and 25th Bengal Infantry; 19th Bengal Lancers, and 1st Punjab Cavalry being the native regiments engaged.

At Kabul the following regiments also saw action: 9th, 67th, 72nd Seaforth Highlanders; 92nd Gordon Highlanders; 9th Lancers. Native regiments: 2nd, 4th, and 5th Goorkas; 5th Punjab Infantry; 23rd and 28th Bengal Infantry; 14th Bengal Lancers, and 12th Bengal Cavalry; 5th Punjab Cavalry; two batteries Punjab Artillery, and the Bengal Sappers and Miners.

Kandahar saw the following troops engaged on 1 September 1880: 7th, 60th, 66th, 72nd, and 92nd; three batteries artillery and the 9th Lancers. Native regiments were at the fore with 1st, 4th, 19th, 28th, and 29th Bombay Infantry; 2nd and 3rd Sikhs; 2nd, 4th, and 5th Goorkas; 15th, 23rd, 24th, and 25th Bengal Infantry; 3rd Bengal, 3rd Bombay, and 3rd Punjab Cavalry; 3rd Scinde Horse; Poona and Central India Horse.

The Afghanistan medal was awarded to the following regiments but without bar: 12th, 14th, 15th, 17th, 25th, 31st, 53rd, 63rd; 6th Dragoon Guards; 8th and 15th Hussars. Signallers from the 65th were also engaged in several actions.

Star for Kabul-Kandahar 1880
Queen Victoria also bestowed a bronze star to all those troops who took part in the 318 mile forced march between 3 and 31 August 1880, from Kabul to Kandahar. This medal takes the form of a

five-pointed star, with small balls between the inner angles, and was struck from the bronze cannon taken at the battle of Kandahar. In the centre is the Imperial monogram v.r.i., encircled by a band with a raised border inscribed KABUL TO KANDAHAR, and the date 1880 below with a sprig of laurel on either side. At the top is the Imperial crown, from which the suspension ring is soldered. The ribbon, 1½in. wide, is rainbow

Khedive's Sudan Medal 1896–1905 (obverse and reverse)

coloured. The reverse is plain with a hollow centre, name and regiment being engraved around the edge in skeleton block letters.

Queen's South Africa medal 1899

This silver medal has the head of Queen Victoria and the legend VICTORIA REGINA ET IMPERATRIX on the obverse. The reverse depicts a standing figure of Britannia grasping the Union Jack in her left hand, while in her right she flourishes a laurel wreath above the heads of the marching troops below.

In the background is the Table Bay with men-of-war; above are the words SOUTH AFRICA. The ribbon has a broad centre stripe of orange, with dark blue and red stripes at the sides; the suspension clasp being silver and plain pattern. There were twenty-six bars issued with this medal reading as follows: CAPE COLONY, NATAL, RHODESIA, RELIEF OF MAFEKING, DEFENCE OF KIMBERLEY, TALANA, ELANDSLAAGTE, DEFENCE OF LADYSMITH, BELMONT, MODDER RIVER, TUGELA HEIGHTS, RELIEF OF KIMBERLEY, PAARDEBERG, ORANGE FREE STATE, RELIEF OF LADYSMITH, DRIEFONTEIN, WEPENER, DEFENCE OF MAFEKING, TRANSVAAL, JOHANNESBURG, LAING'S NEK, DIAMOND HILL, WITTEBERGEN, BELFAST, SOUTH AFRICA 1901, SOUTH AFRICA 1902. These bars should read from the medal upwards in the order as above. The latter two bars were issued to those who, although engaged during the period for which the King's Medal was awarded, were nevertheless not entitled to it by the terms of the grant. One outstanding feature of this medal was the Army Order that decreed that not only the Army, Navy and Colonial forces, but members of the nursing profession could claim it. Bronze medals without bars to authorized camp followers and non-enlisted men are to be found but are very few and far between.

This war was to see, for that day and age, the largest army ever sent out of Great Britain, being some 200,000 men. Her losses in action were 5,774 officers and men, plus 16,168 due to disease and self-inflicted wounds, while another 508 succumbed to their wounds or disease, 22,829 were wounded, and 5,879 being invalided out of the service.

The King's South Africa medal 1902

Authorised in October 1902 by King Edward VII, this medal bears

Queen's and King's South Africa Silver Medals 1899–1902
(obverse and reverse)

his effigy in Field-Marshal's uniform and the legend EDWARDVS VII REX IMPERATOR on the obverse. The reverse is the same as the Queen's SA medal. It was awarded to all those who had served for eighteen months at the front, and still serving on 1 January 1902, or had completed such term before 1 June 1902. Two bars were given; SOUTH AFRICA 1901 and SOUTH AFRICA 1902. The ribbon is composed of three equal stripes of green, white, and orange.

The Mediterranean medal

This medal was awarded to all those who garrisoned the Mediterranean forts during the South Africa War, no bar being issued. Worn with the QSA ribbon the medal is exactly the same as the QSA but has the legend MEDITERRANEAN to the right of Britannia. Most of those engaged in running the forts were from Militia units who volunteered for service abroad during the war.

The Kimberley Star 1900

This award was presented by the Mayor of Kimberley to those who took part in its defence. It took the form of a silver six-pointed star, bearing the hallmark and date letter 'a'. The ribbon is red, white, and blue in the centre, edged with black on one side and yellow on the other. These stars were issued

Distinguished Service Medal. Instituted 1854 (obverse and reverse)

unnamed, and had a variety of suspenders varying from a plain ring to the ornamental. Although highly prized and allowed to be accepted by officers and men, the decoration or its ribbon is not allowed to be worn while in uniform.

The following regiments saw action during the campaign:

CAVALRY: One squadron each of the 1st and 2nd Life Guards and Horse Guards; 1st, 2nd, 3rd, 4th, 5th, 6th, and 7th Dragoon Guards; 1st Dragoons; Scots Greys; 3rd and 4th Hussars; 5th Lancers; 6th Dragoons; 7th and 8th Hussars; 9th Lancers, 10th and 11th Hussars; 16th and 17th Lancers; 18th, 19th and 20th Hussars; and the 21st Lancers.

An interesting photo of 1904 showing the then Lord Lieutenant of Essex distributing the South Africa Medals at Colchester Camp

INFANTRY: Grenadier, Scots, and Coldstream Guards, and the following Line Regiments: Bedfordshire, Berkshire, Border, Cheshire, Cornwall Light Infantry, Derbyshire, Devonshire, Dorsetshire, Durham Light Infantry, Essex, Royal Fusiliers, Gloucestershire, Hampshire, East Kent, West Kent, King's Royal Rifle Corps, Lancashire Fusiliers, East Lancashire, South Lancashire, Loyal North Lancastrian, Royal Lancashire, Liverpool, Leicestershire, Lincoln, Manchester, Middlesex, Norfolk, Northampton, Northumberland Fusiliers, Oxford Light Infantry, Rifle Brigade, Shropshire Light Infantry, Somerset Light Infantry, North and South Staffordshire, Suffolk, Sussex, East and West

Edward VII Long Service Good Conduct Medal 1902–10
(obverse and reverse)

Surrey Regiments, Warwickshire, Wiltshire, Worcestershire, York-
shire, Yorkshire Light Infantry, East and the West Yorkshire, York
and Lancaster, and West Riding Regiments, Argyll and Sutherland
Highlanders, Royal Highlanders ('Black Watch'), Cameron, Sea-
forth and Gordon Highlanders, King's Own Scottish Rifles, Royal
Scots Fusiliers, Scottish Rifles, Highland Light Infantry, Royal
Irish Fusiliers, Royal Dublin Fusiliers, Inniskilling also Munster
Fusiliers, Royal Irish, Royal Irish Rifles, Leinster, Connaught
Rangers, South Wales Borderers, Royal Welsh Fusiliers.

VOLUNTEERS: Thirty-two Battalions of Imperial Yeomanry, City
Volunteer Battalions, Companies, and Corps.

ROYAL HORSE ARTILLERY: A, G, J, M, O, P, Q, R, T, U, and V
Batteries.

ROYAL GARRISON ARTILLERY: Southern Division: 14th, 15th,
16th, and 36th Companies; Eastern Division: 5th, 6th, and 10th
Companies; Western Division: 2nd, 6th, 10th, 14th, 15th, 17th,
and 23rd Companies.

ROYAL FIELD ARTILLERY: 2nd, 4th, 5th, 7th, 8th, 9th, 13th, 14th, 17th, 18th, 19th, 20th, 21st, 28th, 37th, 38th, 39th, 42nd, 43rd, 44th, 53rd, 61st, 62nd, 63rd, 64th, 65th, 66th, 67th, 68th, 69th, 73rd, 74th, 75th, 76th, 77th, 78th, 79th, 81st, 82nd, 83rd, 84th, 85th, 86th, 87th, and 88th Batteries.

Royal Engineers, Army Service and Army Ordnance Corps, Army Veterinary and Army Pay Departments, and RA Medical Corps.

IRREGULAR CORPS: Imperial Light Horse, South African Light Horse, Cape Mounted Rifles, Kitchener's Fighting Scouts, Thorneycroft's Horse, Brabant's Horse, Bethune's Horse, British South African Police, South African Constabulary, National Scouts (Boers), Scottish Horse, Lumsden's Horse and Strathcona's Horse, New South Wales Military Forces, Imperial Bushmen, New Zealand Mounted Rifles and Rough Riders, Queensland Mounted Infantry, South Australian Mounted Infantry and Bushmen's Contingent, Tasmanian Infantry, Artillery, and Bushmen, Victorian Infantry, Victorian Mounted Infantry, Cameron's Scouts, West Australian Contingent, Royal Canadian Dragoons and Batteries of Field Artillery, Canadian Mounted Rifles, Canadian Scouts, Ceylon Mounted Infantry, Bechuanaland Rifles, Border Horse, Border Mounted Rifles, Border Scouts, Brabant's Scouts, British South Africa Police, Cape Cavalry Brigade, Cape Colony Cyclist Corps, Cape Garrison Artillery, Cape Medical Staff Corps, Cape Mounted Rifle Club, Cape Police, 1st City (Grahamstown) Volunteers, Colonial Defence Force, Commander-in-Chief's Bodyguard, Dennison's Scouts, Diamond Field Artillery, Diamond Field Horse, District Mounted Rifles, Driscoll's Scouts, Duke of Edinburgh's Own Volunteer Rifles, Durban Light Infantry, East Griqualand Mounted Rifle Volunteers, Eastern Province Horse, French's Scouts, Frontier Mounted Rifles, Gatacre's Scouts, Herbert District Mounted Rifles, Herchell Mounted Volunteers, Imperial Light Infantry and Light Horse, Johannesburg Mounted Rifles, Kaffrarian Rifles, Kenny's Scouts, Kimberley Regiment, Kimberley Mounted Corps and Light Horse, Kimberley Rifles, Kitchener's Horse, Kuysna Rangers, Komgha Mounted Volunteers, Loch's Horse, Lovat's Scouts, Maritzani Mounted Irregulars, Marshal's Horse, Merre's

Scouts, Military Foot Police, Modder River District Mounted Rifles, Namaqualand Border Scouts, Natal Volunteers, Natal Mounted Infantry, Nesbitt's Horse, New England Mounted Rifles, Orpen's Horse, Pioneer Railway Regiment, Prince Alfred's Own Cape Artillery, Prince Alfred's Volunteer Guard, Prince of Wales' Light Horse, Queenstown Rifle Volunteers, Rand Rifles, Rimington's Guides, Robert's Light Horse, Rundle's Colonial Scouts, Rhodesian Regiment, Scottish Horse, South African Constabulary, South Rhodesian Volunteers, Steinaeker's Horse, Stellenbosch Mounted Infantry, Tembuland Mounted Rifle Corps, Transkei Mounted Rifles, Warwick's Scouts, Western Province Mounted Rifles, Uitenhage Volunteer Rifles, and the Umvoti, Utrecht, Victoria, and Vryburg Mounted Rifles, and Western Light Horse.

TOWN GUARDS: The Aliwal North, Barkly East, Barkly West, Boshof, Burgherdorn, Campell Town, Colesburg, Cradock, Dordrecht District, Douglas, East London, Grahamstown, Griquatown, Hopetown, Hoppesia, Indwe, Jamestown, Kimberley, King Williamstown, Klipdam, Kokstad, Kuruman, Lady Grey, Molteno, Naauwpoort, Port Elizabeth, Queenstown, Qumbu, Starkstroom, Steynsburg, Stormburg, T'somo, Uitenhage, Vryburg, and Warrenton.

These irregular corps formed for just this war are rather unique in the annals of military history because so many of them were struck down by disease or bullets that little or nothing remains of their regiments except their names. Those that did survive have lived on to form the famous South African regiments which fought with such tenacity in both World Wars.

9 naval war medals

Once again it is impossible to list all the Naval medals for every country in a book of this size. Those chosen range from the days of Good Queen Bess, where men had to contend with all the hazards of the sea plus the dangers of handling unstable explosives and equally unstable 'gonnes', to a period (1939) where a man was capable of discharging armour piercing shells from the bowels of a war-ship at the flick of a button.

The most exacting period of naval warfare was that of Nelson's time when the damage inflicted was not so much by the actual cannon or musket ball, but by the thousands of oak splinters sent whistling around the decks once the ball had struck home. So many men were struck down by these wooden missiles that it became the practice to nail complete cow or horse hides over the bulwarks and hatches to try and minimise the danger.

During World War I we had the advent of the 'Q' Ships which sat like decoy ducks awaiting for the stalking U-Boat. Usually these old merchant vessels were crammed from stem to stern with a cargo of cork, planking or wooden crates, in fact anything that helped to keep the old hulk afloat once she had been torpedoed. If the Captain of the U-Boat wanted to complete the *coup de grâce* by surfacing and sinking her by gun-fire he found to his surprise that the stricken ship had 'teeth'. It was the practice to make a great show in abandoning the ship with the crew taking to the life-boats and rafts, then when the submarine was close enough flaps were let down to reveal rows of guns which at that short

range were capable of blowing the U-Boat out of the water. Members of the RN crew who stayed behind to man the guns certainly earned their pay and their medals, for once the German High Command had learnt of this trickery they ordered that vessels acting in a suspicious manner were to be destroyed by torpedoes.

Among the first medals awarded to the navy are those issued by Queen Elizabeth to her Admirals and Commanders who took part in the battle of the 'Wooden Walls' against the 120 mighty galleons of the Spanish Armada in 1588. Spain was to lose over 30,000 men in this conflict with thousands of pounds worth of gold, silver and jewels being sent to the bottom of the sea.

One such medal is on record, in the library at Woburn Abbey, giving out the full details of the medal awarded to Lord Effingham after the defeat of the Armada. These medals were struck in gold and silver and awarded to Marine Commanders as a mark of approbation, and were worn either around the neck suspended by a silver chain, or in the hat.

Drake's medal

This fine example of Elizabethan jewellery presented to Sir Francis Drake by Queen Elizabeth I after his voyage around the world is one of the rarest naval medals known. The frame, set with diamonds and rubies, and enamelled in various colours, forms a beautiful setting for the fine cameo cut in onyx, and is attributed to Valerio Vincenteno. Two heads are carved thereon, one representing Europe cut in the lower strata of white, while out of the upper strata of black the head of a negro has been fashioned. Set in the reverse is a beautiful miniature of Queen Elizabeth by that famous sixteenth century painter Nicholas Hilliard, with the date *Anno Dom: 1575 Regina 20*. From the medal a cluster of baroque pearls connects a pear-shaped drop with the main body of the medal.

Drake was also awarded a jewelled star with twelve points; rubies set in the rays, and diamonds and opals in the circular centre surrounding an orb.

Charles I Naval medals

A medal which was issued to commemorate the launching of the famous three-decker the *Royal Sovereign* in 1637 is described as follows: a portrait of the King in profile looking left; there are varied versions of this medal one of which has the monarch complete with ruff around the neck and a jewel depending from stars on the shoulder; on the other he is shown in armour, with long curling hair over a turn-down collar. The motto CAROLVS ◆ I ◆ D ◆ G ◆ MAG ◆ BRITAIN ◆ FRAN ◆ ET ◆ HIB ◆ REX is around the bust. The date 1639 is on the truncation. The medal is struck in silver and was designed by Nicholas of Bristol.

On the reverse is the *Royal Sovereign* under full sail, and to the left tiny promontories with fortifications; around the ship is the inscription NEC · META · MIHI · QVAE · TERMINUS · ORBI. A smaller medal, believed struck for naval service, was issued with the same inscription.

Charles I 'Royal Sovereign' 1639 (obverse and reverse)

Cromwell Naval medals

Although the Dunbar medal was the first campaign medal as such (1650), the Navy holds the distinction of being the first to be honoured this way in June 1649, when it was decided to issue medals to the officers and men who had 'done good service at sea'. The medal, designed by Thomas Simon, had on the obverse the Parliament in session, and, on the reverse, cartouches depending from the stock of an anchor. The one on the left bears the St George's Cross for England, and that on the right the Harp for Ireland; a rope attached to the anchor is so arranged as to form a decorative surrounding by the arrangement of three twists; above is the word MERUISTI. On the stock of the anchor are the medallist's initials T.S. A word of warning in passing: a number of fakes do exist of these early medals but close inspection for the name or initials of Thomas Simon, (which is always on the genuine pieces) will verify its authenticity.

Wyard medal

This was awarded to Robert Wyard of the *Adventure,* a ship fitted with 22 guns which on the night of 31 July 1650 fought off six royalist frigates. Wyard received a gold medal valued at £50, and his officers and men medals varying in value from £5 to 10s. The obverse is the same as the last but the reverse shows the *Adventure* engaging two of the royalist frigates with the other ships in the

115

background. The inscription which is around the top perimeter reads: SERVICE ◆ DON ◆ AGAINST ◆ SIX ◆ SHIPS ◆ IVLY ◆ Y ◆ XXXI ◆ & AVGVST ◆ Y ◆ I ◆ 1650.

The medal is oval, 1.6in. by 1.35in., and was struck in gold and silver.

Medals for the Dutch Wars

A period when some very finely executed medals were struck and awarded to Admirals participating in the wars which came to a close on 31 July 1653. Several battles had been fought with the Dutch but the major onslaught against the Dutch fleet was enacted on 28 February 1653 when Generals Blake, Deane, and Monk defeated the Dutch under Admirals Van Tromp and De Rutzer, after a three-days' fight off Portland. This was the first official time that soldiers served aboard ship and led to the formation of the Marines. On 31 July 1653 the English chased the Dutch to their own shores where after a terrific fight the enemy lost 26 ships, their Admiral, Van Tromp, and about 6,000 men. The English losses were 2 ships and 1,300 killed and wounded.

The English Parliament rewarded the victors by passing the sum of £2,000 to be spent on chains and medals. Generals Blake and Monk received gold chains valued at £300 each; Vice-Admiral Penn and Rear-Admiral Lawson received chains to the value of £100, and four staff officers received chains worth £40 each. The balance was spent on medals issued among the officers of the fleet.

Four known types of medal were issued. They were struck by the designer, Thomas Simon, who was also responsible for the last group of Commonwealth medals which were struck at the Tower of London under very strict conditions.

Seaman's medal

The seaman's award consists of a small oval medal 0.95in. by 0.85in. with a ring for suspension. Just like the other medals it bears on the obverse an anchor from the stock of which depends two shields bearing respectively the Cross of St George and the Irish harp, encircled by a cable which runs round the whole. Above the anchor stock is MERUISTI (Thou has merited), and on the reverse the House of Commons as on the Dunbar medal.

The Triumph medal

During the fight on 31 July, Admiral Robert Blake's old flagship, the *Triumph,* caught fire. Many of the men jumped overboard; those that remained managed to extinguish the fire and save the ship. For this service the officers and men who stayed with the ship were awarded a special medal with the obverse and reverse exactly the same as on the other medals but with the inscription engraved above the battle scene: FOR EMINENT SERVICE IN SAVING Y TRIUMPH FIRED IN FIGHT WᵇY DVCH in IVLY 1653.

Blake's Jewel

This jewel, thought to have been in the form of a ring, was to reward General Blake for his services in destroying the Spanish fleet off Tenerife on 20 April 1657. A vote in the House of Commons proposed that the sum of £5,000 was to be spent on the jewel which in due course was dispatched to Blake, but whether he ever received it is a matter for conjecture, as he died just within sight of Plymouth on 7 August 1657.

Charles II Naval medals

During October 1665 Charles II declared that a certain percentage of the value of prizes should be paid to those who helped capture them from the Dutch, and that a portion of the proceeds should also be set aside to help the widows of those who died in battle, to assist the sick and the wounded, and to provide medals for those who performed special service.

With the 'war drums' sounding once more against the Dutch in February 1665, by 3 June the Dutch fleet was engaged and beaten by the English fleet under Prince Rupert, the Duke of York, and Admirals Lawson and Penn. To commemorate this victory, medals were issued in gold and silver. One bore on the obverse the bust of Charles with his titles, and on the reverse the island of Great Britain with the legend QUATUOR MARIA VINDICO. A smaller medal has on the obverse a triumphal chariot drawn by sea-horses, with the King seated therein, with the legend ET PONTUS SERVIET.

In 1665 Charles II also issued a large circular silver medal some 2in. in diameter with the motto PRO TALIBVS AVIS (for such enterprises) in the exergue of the reverse, which depicts a battle at

Charles II Silver Naval Medal 1665 (obverse and reverse)

sea with a wreck in the foreground and Charles looking on at the engagement dressed as a Roman General. Struck by that famous medallist Röttier, this is a fine example of his work and as it was undated is thought to have been issued for any of the sea-battles during that period.

The La Hogue medals 1692

This battle which united the English and Dutch fleets together against the French lasted five days and ended in a crushing defeat for the French. Several medals designed by Röttier were ordered to be struck by Queen Mary, who expressed her satisfaction in the result of the conflict by distributing £30,000 among the soldiers and sailors who had been engaged in the battle.

One of the most important medals, 1.95in. in diameter, was struck in gold and silver: it bears on the obverse the busts of William III and Mary II, the King dressed in Roman armour and wearing long hair, the Queen simply draped. Around the conjoined busts the inscription GVL: ET: MAR: D: G: B: F: ET: H: REX: REGINA; and on the reverse the representation of the French Admiral's flagship, *Le Soleil Royal*, in flames. This ship was, with three others, driven ashore and set on fire by English fireships. Above the scene is the legend NOX · NVLLA · SECVTA · EST (No Night Followed), and in the exergue PVGN: NAV: ANG: ET · FR: 21 · MAY · 1692.

One of the medals in gold, together with a chain valued at £50 was presented to Captain John Tupper 'for the good services performed by him' when in a dense fog he sailed through the French fleet and brought news of their presence to Admiral Russell at Spithead.

It was after this victory that Queen Mary founded the Greenwich Hospital as a home for seamen disabled while in the service of their country.

Another unusual gold medal struck during this reign for service at sea was awarded to Captain Peter Jolliffe, master of the *Sea Adventure* hoy, with the following inscription on the reverse: *His Maties' Gift as a reward to Peter Jollif, of Poole, for his good service ag^t the enemy in retaking a ketch of Weymouth from a French Privateer, and chaceing the said Privateer on Shoar* *near Lulworth in ye Isle of Purbeck, where shee was broken in pieces, 1694.*

A rather outstanding award was bestowed upon the master of a fishing smack, William Thompson who, with one man and a boy armed with a couple of small guns and a few muskets, attacked, on 30 May 1695, a French privateer well armed with two cannon and manned by sixteen seamen, which he defeated and captured after two hours' fighting. He was also allowed to retain the prize ship.

Queen Anne's Lamprière Gold medal

In 1703, Captain James Lamprière was awarded a gold medal with the following inscription engraved upon the reverse· *Her Maj^{ties} reward to Capt. James Lamprière for his Zeal to her Service, and his Successful Conducting ye Squadron commanded by Rear Admiral Dilkes, who destroyed a considerable number of ye Enemy's Merchant Ships under convey of 3 Men of War on their own coast.* Below this inscription on a ribbon the Arms of Lamprière together with the motto TRUE · TO · MY · TRUST. On the obverse is the bust of Queen Anne, facing left, wearing the Royal Crown and Star of the Order of the Garter, surrounded by the legend ANNA · DEI · GRATIA · MAG : BRITAN : FRA : ET · HIB : REGINA.

Queen Anne's Boy's Medal for Gallantry

This award is unique and needless to say very valuable indeed. It was struck on the orders of Queen Anne and awarded to a young boy for gallantry. The obverse bears the laureated bust of Anne facing left, draped, with a row of pearls about the shoulders with the legend ANNA D : G : MAG : BRI : FR : ET : HIB : REG : . On the reverse is the inscription: *Her Maj^{ties} reward to Robert Taylor Boy of ye Mary Galley, for his Zeal and Courage at ye taking of ye French Privateer Jacques La Blonde of Dunkirk.*

The medal which has a raised border of laurel leaves and roses, and a ring for suspension, is 2.75in. in diameter.

It is interesting to note that in a declaration made on 1 June 1702, Queen Anne stated that in future the cost of providing these medals was to be paid out of her share of the prize monies.

Although not an official award, the medal awarded to Captain Matthew Martin, Commander of the *Marlborough*, for the gallant defence of his ship against three French war-ships in the Bay of Bengal and getting her safely to Fort St George in the year 1712, is really something outstanding in the line of medals. It bore on the obverse the arms of the East India Company, and was enamelled and set with diamonds; the reverse was engraved setting out the deeds for which it was awarded. Captain Martin was awarded £1,000 sterling as well.

Admiral Vernon medal 1739

Commemorative medals were also struck in connection with the taking of Puerto Bello, in the Caribbean Sea, by Admiral Vernon with six ships in 1739, after a forty-eight hour bombardment which destroyed all the city's fortifications. There were several 'Vernon' medals struck, varying in size and shape, in silver, bronze, and german-silver; but nearly all bearing on the reverse: *He took Porto Bello with Six Ships only.*

Callis Gold medal 1742

This Gold medal and chain, valued at £100, was awarded to Captain Smith Callis RN for taking his fireship *Duke* into the Port of St Tropez in Provence and burning five Royal Spanish galleys on 14 June 1742. On the obverse of the medal, which is 2.1in. in diameter, George II, laureated and attired as a Roman Emperor, is represented in the act of presenting a medal to an officer. Under the group, at the top of the plain exergue, is the medallist's name T. PINGO F:. Above all on a ribbon is PROTALIBVS AVSIS (for such enterprise). On the reverse are five galleys inshore with a squadron of ships-of-war preparing to attack, in the exergue OB.V. TRIREM. HISPAN. A.S. CALLIS. COMBVST. V. IVLII. MDCCXLII. This date on the medal is the day the news of the successful venture reached London. It is believed that the silver medal was awarded to the other officer who took part in the action.

Hornby Medal and Chain 1744

Another gold medal and chain at a cost of £100 was ordered by the King on 18 September 1744, to be awarded to Captain Richard Hornby, of the *Wrightson and Isabella* of Sunderland, plus a bounty of £5 to each of his five men and 40s to each of his three boys, for having fought and sank after a five hour battle a French privateer armed with ten cannon and eight swivel guns, and manned by seventy-five seamen.

Louisbourg 1753

Medals by T. Pingo, with rings for suspension, were struck in gold, silver and bronze for those who had distinguished themselves at the taking of Louisbourg on 26 July 1753. Generals in charge of the land operations were Amherst and Wolfe, and at sea, Admiral Boscawen. Four specimens of the gold medal were in existence during the early part of this century. One was in the Montague collection and another was sold at Sotheby's in 1895. The third one was awarded to Sir Alexander Schomberg, and the fourth to Senior Midshipman (afterwards Sir George) Young.

The Glorious 1st of June Navy Gold medal

This battle which was fought off Ushant, when Admiral Lord Howe gained his great victory against the French, will always be remembered by medal collectors if only because it heralded the first regulation medal for naval service. Two medals were struck, a 2in. diameter one in gold for admirals and a smaller version measuring $1\frac{1}{2}$in. in diameter for lesser ranks. They were hung from a wire bar and ring and suspended by the white, blue-edged ribbon through a button-hole on the left breast.

Distributed on 9 November 1796, this medal bears on the obverse an antique galley on the prow of which the winged figure of Victory is shown placing a wreath upon the head of Britannia, who stands with her right foot on a Greek helmet; in her left hand she holds a spear; beside her is an oval shield bearing the Union Jack. The reverse is very much the same for both medals with the name of the recipient and the event engraved in the centre. The larger medals have a wreath of oak and laurel around the inscription which is omitted from the smaller medals.

These medals were instituted in 1794 and continued until 1815. The total number of gold medals issued was 140, of which eight were Admirals' medals awarded with chains; flag officers were issued with broad ribbons for suspension from the neck, and 117 were of the captains' size ($1\frac{1}{2}$in.). Gold chains were only awarded with the Admirals' medals for 1 June.

Among the ships engaged at the battle were the *Queen Charlotte, Royal Sovereign, Royal George, Barfleur, Bellerophon, Impregnable, Queen, Caesar, Culloden, Defence, Glory, Gibraltar, Invincible, Majestic, Leviathan, Marlborough, Montague, Ramillies, Russell, Orion, Thunderer, Tremendous, Audacious, Alfred, Brunswick* and *Valiant,* the frigates *Aquilon, Latona, Phaeton, Niger, Southampton, Venus, Charon* and *Pegasus,* the sloops *Comet* and *Incendiary,* and the cutters *Ranger* and *Rattler.*

Among those badly damaged was the British Admiral's flagship, the *Queen Charlotte,* also the *Brunswick, Defence* and *Marlborough.* It is interesting to note that detachments of the 2nd, 25th and 69th Foot also served as Marines during this famous sea battle.

Davison's Medal for the Nile 1798
Lord Nelson captured so much booty that he employed a prize agent, Mr Alexander Davison, to handle the disposal of the many choice items that came his way. The rewards must have been high because we find Mr Davison presenting a medal to every officer and seaman of Nelson's fleet; gold to captains and lieutenants, silver to warrant officers, bronze gilt to petty officers, and bronze to seamen and marines.

Upon the edge is impressed FROM ALEXANDER DAVISON ESQ., ST. JAMES SQUARE: A TRIBUTE OF REGARD. This medal modelled by C. H. Küchler, $1\frac{7}{8}$in. in diameter, was issued unnamed, but many recipients had their names together with the name of their ship engraved above the sky-line on the reverse. Although they were worn suspended from a broad blue ribbon, they were not officially sanctioned.

On the obverse there is a standing figure of Britannia holding aloft in her right hand a branch, while tucked under her left arm is a rather outsize shield bearing the profile of Nelson. The wording REAR ADMIRAL LORD NELSON OF THE NILE stretches around the outer surface. The reverse depicts nearly thirty ships manoeuvering into battle positions with the sun on the horizon

123

spreading its rays to the sky; in the exergue is VICTORY OF THE NILE AUGUST I. I. 1798, and above the battle scene on a ribbon, ALMIGHTY GOD HAS BLESSED HIS MAJESTY'S ARMS.

After the death of Lord Nelson at Trafalgar, at 4.30 p.m. on 21 October 1805, we have two unofficial medals struck to commemorate this last and greatest of Nelson's victories. One was struck by Matthew Boulton, of the famous Soho Mint near Birmingham; the other being ordered by Davison, to be distributed among the surviving members of the crew of the *Victory*.

Boulton's medal, which was $1\frac{7}{8}$in. in diameter, was struck in silver for senior officers, and in pewter for junior officers and seamen. On the edge of the medal is the inscription: TO THE HEROES OF TRAFALGAR FROM M. BOULTON. The obverse has a fine bust of Nelson with the inscription HORATIO VISCOUNT NELSON. K.B. OF BRONTE; while on the reverse the battle is represented *en cameo* with the famous signal: ENGLAND EXPECTS EVERY MAN TO DO HIS DUTY, on a ribbon, and in the exergue TRAFALGAR OCT. 21 1805.

Boulton may have meant well, but to the common seamen it was more of an insult, so much so that it is on record that many of the medals were tossed contemptuously into the sea! There were a few proofs struck in bronze.

The two medals ordered by Alexander Davison were 2in. in diameter and struck in pewter or german-silver, and are sometimes found framed in gold, silver or gilt rims, with a loop for suspension from a blue ribbon.

The obverse has a shield bearing the Arms of Nelson, encircled by a garter inscribed TRIA · JUNCTO · IN · UNO · ensigned by a bust of Viscount Nelson. A laurel branch is to the left, and a palm branch to the right, and on a scroll beneath the shield: PALMAM QUI MERUIT FERAT and the double inscription: ADMIRAL LORD NELSON D. OF BRONTE NATUS SEP. 29th 1758. HOSTE DEVICTO REQUIEVIT OCT. 21st 1805 and ENGLAND EXPECTS EVERY MAN WILL DO HIS DUTY. On the reverse is a man-of-war with sails furled, and above: THE LORD IS A MAN OF WAR, EXODUS C 15 v 3, while below is: VICTORY OFF TRAFALGAR OVER THE COMBINED FLEETS OF FRANCE & SPAIN OCT. 21 1805. Beneath the man-of-war is: HALLIDAY FECIT.

124

The following ships were engaged in the battle: *Victory, Royal Sovereign, Temeraire, Britannia, Conqueror, Neptune, Agamemnon, Leviathan, Ajax, Africa, Minotaur, Orion, Belleisle, Mars, Thunderer, Spartiate, Bellerophon, Achille, Colossus, Polyphemus, Revenge, Dreadnought, Swiftsure, Defence, Defiance, Prince,* and *Tonnant,* the frigates *Sirius, Phoebe, Euryalus,* and *Naiad,* the cutter *Entreprenaute* and the schooner *Pickle.*

Thus we come to the official medal – the Naval General Service – which had 230 bars issued between the years 1793 and 1840. Many of the bars carry the names of the action, others have just BOAT SERVICE which commemorates the brilliant acts by boats' crews of capturing enemy vessels, or recovering British ships lost to the enemy. Bars granted for Boat Service are as follows:

15 March 1793 – 1 only issued; 17 March 1794 – 30 issued; 29 May 1797 – 3 issued; 9 June 1799 – 4 issued; 20 December 1799 – 3 issued; 29 July 1800 – 4 issued; 29 August 1800 – 26 issued; 27 October 1800 – 5 issued; 21 July 1801 – 9 issued; 27 June 1803 – 5 issued; 4 November 1803 – 1 issued; 4 February 1804 – 10 issued; 4 June 1805 – 10 issued; 16 July 1806 – 51 issued; 2 January 1807 – 2 issued; 21 January 1807 – 9 issued; 19 April 1807 – 1 issued; 13 February 1808 – 3 issued; 10 July 1808 – 8 issued; 11 August 1808 – 12 issued; 28 November 1808 – 2 issued; 7 July 1809 – 33 issued; 14 July 1809 – 8 issued; 25 July 1809 – 35 issued; 27 July 1809 – 10 issued; 29 July 1809 – 11 issued; 28 August 1809 – 14 issued; 1 November 1809 – 117 issued; 13 December 1809 – 10 issued; 13 February 1810 – 17 issued; 1 May 1810 – 18 issued; 28 June 1810 – 24 issued; 27 September 1810 – 34 issued; 4 November 1810 – 2 issued; 23 November 1810 – 66 issued; 24 December 1810 – 6 issued; 4 May 1811 – 10 issued; 30 July 1811 – 4 issued; 2 August 1811 – 10 issued; 20 September 1811 – 8 issued; 4 December 1811 – 18 issued; 4 April 1812 – 4 issued; 1 September 1812 and 18 September 1812 – 24 issued for these 2 clasps; 17 September 1812 – 11 issued; 29 September 1812 – 26 issued; 6 January 1813 – 21 issued; 21 March 1813 – 6 issued; 28 April 1813 – 2 issued; April and May 1813 – 54 issued; 2 May 1813 – 49

issued; 8 April 1814 – 23 issued; 24 May 1814 – 11 issued; 3 and 6 September 1814 – 1 issued; 14 December 1814 – 117 issued. The last two bars are for actions in the war with America.

1914–18 Mercantile Marine War medal

This was a medal which was granted to the British, Dominion, Colonial and Indian Mercantile Marine for those who had served at sea not less than six months between 4 August 1914 and 11 November 1918. Among those included were; licensed pilots, post office cable ships, and fishermen and crews of pilotage and lighthouse vessels. However, all the recipients must have served at sea, and not in harbours, rivers, or other inland waters. This medal could also be issued posthumously to the next of kin.

The medal is of bronze and bears George v's bust on the

obverse with the usual legend. It has a plain, straight suspender bar with a red and green, white central striped ribbon. The reverse depicts a merchant ship fighting through an angry sea; a sinking submarine, and in the background a sailing ship. The number, name, rank and ship are engraved around the edge.

Atlantic Star 1939–45
This bronze star, suspended from a 1¼in. wide, blue, white and sea green ribbon, was awarded to those serving in the RN between 3 September 1939 and 8 May 1945, in the Atlantic or Home Waters. Personnel employed with the convoys to North Russia and in the South Atlantic were eligible provided that the 1939–45 Star had first been earned for six months operational service. Air crews also qualified if they had taken part in active operations against the enemy in the areas specified and within the dates stated; but subject to eight weeks service in an operational unit, and the prior award of the 1939–45 bronze Star. This, like the other bronze Stars of World War II is plain one side with the Royal cypher and name of campaign within a circle on the other.

Pacific Star
Granted for operational service in the Pacific from 8 December 1941. The normal bronze Star is worn from a ribbon of dark green with red edges, a central yellow stripe and stripes of dark blue and light blue.

Those serving with the Royal Navy and Merchant Navy in the Pacific Ocean, the Indian Ocean and the South China sea qualified, likewise RN shore personnel, air crews and RAF ground personnel. Territories for land service eligibility as follows: Hong Kong, Malaya, Nauru, Ocean Island, Gilbert and Ellice Islands, Borneo and Sarawak, Celebes, Bismark Archipelago, Molucca Islands, Solomon Islands (British Solomon Islands and Australian Mandated Territory), Sumatra, Timor, Java, New Guinea.

USA Navy Cross
First established in 1919, this cross could be awarded to anyone in the Naval service who, since 6 April 1917 had 'distinguished himself by extraordinary heroism or distinguished service in the

J*

line of his profession, in cases where such heroism or distinguished service is not of a character to justify the award of the Medal of Honor or DSM'.

In August 1942 these rules were altered thus giving the decoration precedence over the Navy DSM thereby making it for combat duty only.

This medal consists of a dark bronze cross with points of laurel at the junction of the limbs. The centre of the reverse bears crossed anchors with the letters 'USN', and the obverse the design of a caravel (light sailing ship). The ribbon has a white centre with navy-blue and dark-blue edges. The Navy Cross has been awarded to officers and men of Navies allied to the USA. Further acts of gallantry are marked by a gold star worn upon the ribbon.

USA Distinguished Service medal (Navy)

This medal is in gilded bronze, with the obverse bearing the American eagle in the centre standing proud and facing left. It is surrounded by a blue-enamelled circle bearing the words · UNITED · STATES · OF · AMERICA · NAVY · and a gold wave scroll border. On the reverse is a trident within a laurel wreath surrounded by a blue circle with the words FOR DISTINGUISHED SERVICE. The suspender mounting is a white enamelled star with rays issuing from between the limbs; a gold anchor is surmounted upon the star. The ribbon is of blue and yellow. A gold star is worn upon the ribbon if the recipient performs further acts to justify the award of another medal.

USA Commendation Ribbon (Navy)

This is the equivalent to the British 'Mentioned in Despatches' and is awarded by the Secretary of the Navy or the Commander of Atlantic or Pacific fleets for acts not sufficiently high enough to warrant the award of a silver Star. The ribbon is green with white stripes towards the edges.

USA Civil War 1861–5

Although this is known as the Civil War medal it was not authorised for the Navy until 1908. The obverse has a representation of the fight between those famous iron-clad ships *Monitor* and

Merrimae, and the words THE CIVIL WAR, 1861–5. The reverse has an eagle standing proud upon an anchor and cable over the words FOR SERVICE with sprays of oak and laurel beneath. The words UNITED STATES NAVY or UNITED STATES MARINE CORPS (whatever the case may be) are found around the top circumference. The ribbon is half dark blue, half grey.

USA Dewey medal 1898

For the battle of Manila Bay, which took place on 1 May 1898, a bronze medal was authorised by Congress on 3 June 1898 to be awarded to all officers and men engaged in the battle. The obverse bears the bust of Commodore Dewey in uniform and the inscription, *The Gift of the People of the United States to the Officers and Men of the Asiatic Squadron under the Command of Commodore George Dewey,* on the field to the left and right of him. The reverse depicts a finely modelled figure of a gunner sitting on a naval gun with the American flag draped across his knees. Beneath his left foot is a small panel upon which the name of one of the six ships is stamped. Encircling this scene is the record IN MEMORY OF THE VICTORY OF MANILA BAY. MAY 1st. 1898. This medal, designed by the famous American sculptor, Daniel Chester French, and struck by Messrs Tiffany & Co. was to commemorate the crushing blow inflicted upon the Spanish navy during the Spanish-American War when, with only six ships, the USN destroyed the fleet of eleven Spanish battleships in Manila Bay without the loss of a single man! The ribbon, $1\frac{1}{2}$in. wide, is yellow with broad edges of blue.

USA Naval Presidential Unit Citations

In February 1942 the system of unit citations was introduced for the Army and Navy and US Marine Corps. This was to be awarded to any ship, aircraft or Naval unit, or any Marine Corps aircraft, detachment or higher unit, for outstanding performances in action. In the case of a ship the insignia takes the form of a blue, yellow and scarlet burgee pendant worn in a prominent position. There is also a bronze plaque bearing the citation insignia, with the citation engraved beneath to be displayed upon ships, aircraft units, tank units, etc. during time of war.

Belgium Maritime Decoration

Established during World War I (1918), it was awarded to seamen for devotion to duty. Two crosses were struck: first and second class, in gold and silver and white enamel, with a monogram 'A' in the centre, and swords in the angles. There are three medals in gold, silver and bronze with crossed swords at the top for three lower classes. The ribbon is the same for all classes being sea-green, with two groups of five narrow stripes of red, yellow, black, yellow, red. Anchors crossed are worn on the ribbon in the same metal as the cross or medal.

Belgium Maritime medal 1940–5

Awarded for the same services as the 1918 version this bronze medal bears the rampant lion of Belgium on the obverse and the Royal monogram on the reverse. It has a ring for suspending the sea-green and white striped ribbon which also carries a pair of crossed anchors. An interesting point regarding these awards is the fact that most of them have to be purchased by the recipient himself as they were not supplied by the Government.

Greek Order of Naval Commandos

Granted by Royal Decree 3 March 1948 in recognition of the Royal appreciation of the conduct of those officers, petty officers and men who boarded ships of the Royal Hellenic navy whose crews had mutinied on 22–23 April 1944, in the port of Alexandria. These commandos successfully quelled the mutiny and brought the crews back to duty. The bronze Order which has no ribbon is worn just below the left breast pocket, and consists of a full wreath of laurels surmounted by the Royal Crown, a pair of crossed swords, and four small crowns in each quarter.

USSR. The Order of Ushakov (Navy)

There are two classes of this Order, 1st Class being in gold, and 2nd Class in silver. They consist of a five-pointed star on which is a large silver anchor. Over the shank and resting on the arms are chain and rope circles within which, on a pale blue ground, is a portrait of Admiral Ushakov in Naval uniform with decorations. The 1st Class has the portrait in silver; on the 2nd Class it is gold.

The Order is worn on the right breast, but when ribbons alone are worn they are respectively light blue with two broad white stripes, and white with two light blue stripes. The Medal of Ushakov consists of the centre medallion and anchor which hangs from a V-shaped chain from a ribbon of light blue with dark blue and white stripes.

USSR. *The Order of Nakimov (Navy)*

Once again there are two classes of this Order, 1st Class in gold, and 2nd Class in silver. They consist of a five-pointed star, between the points of which are anchors, the shanks split and containing red triangles. The centre bears a profile of Admiral Nakimov wearing a peaked cap. The portrait for the 1st Class is on a bright blue, while for the 2nd Class it is all silver.

The Medal of Nakimov is gold and consists of the portrait described previously. It hangs from a light blue ribbon with three white stripes in the centre, while the ribbons for the Order are 1st Class, black with two broad orange stripes and 2nd Class, orange with two black stripes.

The naval awards bestowed upon the Imperial German and Third German Reich will be found in Chapter 6, 'Medals of Germany'.

10 regimental designations through the ages

Name at Formation	Title Changes Cavalry
Life Guards	1st & 2nd
Royal Horse Guards	The 'Blues'
1st Dragoon Guards	The King's
2nd Dragoon Guards	Queen's Bays
3rd Dragoon Guards	Prince of Wales'
4th Dragoon Guards	Royal Irish
5th Dragoon Guards	Princess Charlotte of Wales
6th Dragoon Guards	Carabineers
7th Dragoon Guards	Princess Royal's
1st Dragoons	Royal
2nd Dragoons	Royal North British (Scots Greys)
3rd Hussars	Light Dragoons
4th Hussars	Light Dragoons
5th Lancers	Royal Irish
6th Dragoons	Inniskilling
7th Hussars	Light Dragoons
8th Hussars	Light Dragoons
9th Lancers	Light Dragoons
10th Hussars	Light Dragoons
11th Hussars	Light Dragoons
12th Lancers	Light Dragoons
13th Hussars	Light Dragoons

1915 Title	Present Title
Same	Same
Same	Same
Same	1st Queen's Dragoon Guards
Same	1st Queen's Dragoon Guards
Same	3rd Carabineers
Same	4th/7th Royal Dragoon Guards
Same	5th Royal Inniskilling Dragoon Guards
Same	3rd Carabineers
Same	4th/7th Royal Dragoon Guards
Same	The Royal Dragoons
Royal Scots Greys	Same
The King's Own	The Queen's Own Hussars
The Queen's Own	The Queen's Royal Irish Hussars
Same	16th/5th The Queen's Royal Lancers
Same	5th Royal Inniskilling Dragoon Guards
The Queen's Own	The Queen's Own Hussars
King's Royal Irish	The Queen's Royal Irish Hussars
The Queen's Royal	9th/12th Royal Lancers
Prince of Wales' Own	10th Royal Hussars
Prince Albert's Own	11th Hussars
Prince of Wales'	Royal. 9th/12th Royal Lancers
None	13th/18th Royal Hussars

133

Name at Formation	Title Changes Cavalry
14th Hussars	The King's
15th Hussars	Light Dragoons
16th Lancers	The Queen's
17th Lancers	'Death or Glory Boys'
18th Hussars	Light Dragoons
19th Hussars	1st Bengal European Cav.
20th Hussars	2nd Bengal European Cav.
21st Lancers	3rd Bengal European Cav.

Name at Formation	Title Changes Infantry
Grenadier Guards	1st 2nd 3rd Battalions
Coldstream Guards	1st & 2nd Battalions
Scots Fusilier Guards	1st & 2nd Battalions
Irish Guards	
Welsh Guards	
1st Regt	The Royal
2nd Regt	Queen's Royal
3rd Regt	East Kent – The Buffs
4th Regt	King's Own Royal
5th Regt	Northumberland Fusiliers
6th Regt	Royal 1st Warwickshire
7th Regt	Royal Fusiliers
8th Regt	The King's
9th Regt	East Norfolk
10th Regt	North Lincolnshire
11th Regt	North Devonshire
12th Regt	East Suffolk
13th Regt	Prince Albert's Light Inf.
14th Regt	Buckinghamshire

1915 Title	Present Title
Same	14th/20th King's Hussars
The King's	15th/19th The King's Royal Hussars
Same	16th/5th The Queen's Royal Lancers
Duke of Cambridge's Own	17th/21st Lancers
Queen Mary's Own	13th/18th Royal Hussars
Princess of Wales' Own	15th/19th The King's Royal Hussars
	14th/20th The King's Royal Hussars
Empress of India's	17th/21st Lancers

1915 Title	Present Title
Same	Same
Same	Same
Same	Scots Guards
Same	Irish Guards
Same	Welsh Guards
Royal Scots (Lothian Regt)	Lowland Brigade
Royal West Surrey Regt	The Queen's Regt
East Kent Regt	The Queen's Regt
Royal Lancaster Regt	The King's Own Royal Border Regt
Same	The Royal Regt of Fusiliers
Royal Warwickshire Regt	The Royal Regt of Fusiliers
City of London Regt	The Royal Regt of Fusiliers
Liverpool Regt	The King's Regt
Norfolk Regt	The Royal Anglian Regt
Lincolnshire Regt	The Royal Anglian Regt
Devonshire Regt	The Devonshire & Dorset Regt
Suffolk Regt	The Royal Anglian Regt
Prince Albert's (Somersetshire Light Inf.)	The Light Infantry
Prince of Wales' Own (West Yorkshire Regt)	The Prince of Wales' Own Regt of Yorkshire

Name at Formation	Title Changes Infantry
15th Regt	Yorkshire, East Riding
16th Regt	The Bedfordshire
17th Regt	Leicestershire
18th Regt	Royal Irish
19th Regt	1st Yorkshire, N. Riding
20th Regt	East Devonshire
21st Regt	Royal North British Fusiliers
22nd Regt	The Cheshire
23rd Regt	Royal Welsh Fusiliers
24th Regt	2nd Warwickshire
25th Regt	King's Own Borderers
26th Regt	The Cameronian
27th Regt	Inniskilling
28th Regt	North Gloucestershire
29th Regt	Worcestershire
30th Regt	Cambridgeshire
31st Regt	Huntingdonshire
32nd Regt	Cornwall Light Inf.
33rd Regt	Duke of Wellington's
34th Regt	Cumberland
35th Regt	Royal Sussex
36th Regt	Herefordshire
37th Regt	North Hampshire
38th Regt	1st Staffordshire
39th Regt	Dorsetshire
40th Regt	2nd Somersetshire
41st Regt	The Welch
42nd Regt	Royal Highland (Black Watch)
43rd Regt	Monmouthshire Light Inf.
44th Regt	East Essex

1915 Title	Present Title
East Yorkshire Regt	The Prince of Wales' Own
Bedfordshire Regt	The Royal Anglian Regt
Leicestershire Regt	The Royal Anglian Regt
Royal Irish Regt	Disbanded
Alexandra, Princess of Wales' Own (Yorkshire Regt)	The Green Howard's
The Lancashire Fusiliers	The Royal Regt of Fusiliers
Royal Scots Fusiliers	Royal Highland Fusiliers
Cheshire Regt	The Cheshire Regt
Same	Same
South Wales Borderers	Same
King's Own Scottish Borderers	Same
1st Cameronians (Scottish Rifles)	The Cameronians
1st Royal Inniskilling Fusiliers	The Royal Irish Rangers
1st Gloucestershire Regt	The Gloucestershire Regt
1st Worcestershire Regt	Worcestershire Regt
1st E. Lancashire Regt	Disbanded
1st E. Surrey Regt.	The Queen's Regt
1st Duke of Cornwall's Light Inf.	The Light Inf.
1st West Riding Regt	The Duke of Wellington's Regt
1st Border Regt	The King's Own Royal Border Regt
1st Royal Sussex	The Queen's Regt
2nd Worcestershire Regt	
1st Hampshire Regt	The Royal Hampshire Regt
1st S. Staffordshire Regt	The Staffordshire Regt
1st Dorsetshire Regt	The Devonshire & Dorset Regt
Prince of Wales' Volunteers 1st S. Lancashire Regt	Lancashire Brigade
1st Welch Regt	The Welch Regt
1st Black Watch (Royal Highlanders)	The Black Watch
1st Oxfordshire Light Inf.	The Royal Green Jackets
1st Essex Regt	The Royal Anglian Regt

Name at Formation	Title Changes Infantry
45th Regt	Nottinghamshire (Sherwood Foresters)
46th Regt	South Devonshire
47th Regt	Lancashire
48th Regt	Northamptonshire
49th Regt	Princess Charlotte of Wales'
50th Regt	The Queen's Own
51st Regt	2nd Yorkshire, West Riding (King's Own Light Inf.)
52nd Regt	Oxfordshire Light Inf.
53rd Regt	Shropshire
54th Regt	West Norfolk
55th Regt	Westmorland
56th Regt	West Essex
57th Regt	West Middlesex
58th Regt	Rutlandshire
59th Regt	2nd Nottinghamshire
60th Regt	King's Royal Rifle Corps
61st Regt	South Gloucestershire
62nd Regt	Wiltshire
63rd Regt	West Suffolk
64th Regt	2nd Staffordshire
65th Regt	2nd Yorkshire, N. Riding
66th Regt	Berkshire
67th Regt	South Hampshire
68th Regt	Durham Light Inf.
69th Regt	South Lincolnshire
70th Regt	Surrey
71st Regt	Highland Light Inf.
72nd Regt	Duke of Albany's Own Highlanders

1915 *Title*	*Present Title*
1st Sherwood Foresters	
(Derbyshire Regt)	The Sherwood Foresters
2nd Duke of Cornwall's Light	
Inf.	The Light Inf.
1st Royal N. Lancashire Regt	The Loyal Regt
1st Northamptonshire Regt	The Royal Anglian Regt
1st Royal Berks. Regt	The Duke of Edinburgh's Royal Regt
1st Royal West Kent Regt	The Queen's Regt
1st King's Own	
(Yorkshire Light Inf.)	The Light Inf.
2nd Oxfordshire Light Inf.	The Royal Green Jackets
1st The King's (Shropshire	
Light Inf.)	The Light Inf.
2nd Dorsetshire	The Devonshire & Dorset Regt
2nd The Border	The King's Own Royal Border Regt
2nd Essex	The Royal Anglian Regt
1st Duke of Cambridge's Own	
(Middlesex)	The Queen's Regt
2nd Northamptonshire	The Royal Anglian Regt
2nd East Lancashire	The Lancashire Regt
Same	The Royal Green Jackets
2nd Gloucestershire	The Gloucestershire Regt
1st Duke of Edin. (Wilts.)	The Duke of Edinburgh's Royal Regt
1st Manchester	The King's Regt
1st Prince of Wales (N. Staffs.)	The Mercian Brigade
1st Yorkshire & Lancaster	The York & Lanc. Regt
2nd Princess Charlotte of	
Wales' (Royal Berks.)	
2nd Hampshire	The Royal Hampshire Regt
1st Durham Light Inf.	
2nd Welsh	
2nd East Surrey	The Queen's Regt
1st Highland Light Inf.	
1st Seaforth Highlanders	
Ross-shire Buffs (Duke of Albany's)	

Name at Formation	Title Changes Infantry
73rd Regt	Perthshire
74th Regt	Highland Regt
75th Regt	Stirlingshire Regt
76th Regt	None
77th Regt	East Middlesex
78th Regt	Highland Regt (Ross-shire Buffs)
79th Regt	Cameron Highlanders
80th Regt	Staffordshire Vol.
81st Regt	Loyal Lincoln Vol.
82nd Regt	Prince of Wales' Vol.
83rd Regt	County Dublin
84th Regt	York & Lancaster
85th Regt	Bucks Vol. (King's Light Inf.)
86th Regt	Royal County Down
87th Regt	Royal Irish Fusiliers
88th Regt	Connaught Rangers
89th Regt	Princess Victoria's
90th Regt	Perthshire Vol. (Light Inf.)
91st Regt	Argyllshire Highlanders
92nd Regt	Gordon Highlanders
93rd Regt	Sutherland Highlanders
94th Regt	None

1915 Title	*Present Title*
2nd Black Watch (Royal Highlanders)	
2nd Highland Light Inf.	The Royal Highland Fusiliers
1st Gordon Highlanders	The Gordon Highlanders
2nd Duke of Wellington's (West Riding)	The Duke of Wellington's Regt
2nd Duke of Cambridge's Own (Middlesex)	The Queen's Regt
2nd Seaforth Highlanders (Ross-shire Buffs) Duke of Albany's	The Queen's Own Highlanders
Queen's Own Cameron Highlanders	The Queen's Own Highlanders
2nd South Staffordshire	The Staffordshire Regt
2nd Loyal N. Lancaster	The Loyal Regt
2nd Prince of Wales' Vol. (South Lanc.)	The Lancashire Regt
1st Royal Irish Rifles	The Royal Irish Rangers
2nd York & Lancaster	The York & Lanc. Regt
2nd The King's (Shropshire Light Inf.)	The Light Inf.
2nd Royal Irish Rifles	The Royal Irish Rangers
1st Princess Victoria's (Royal Irish Fusiliers)	The Royal Irish Rangers
1st Connaught Rangers	Disbanded
2nd Princess Victoria's (Royal Irish Fusiliers)	Royal Irish Rangers
2nd Cameronians (Scottish Rifles)	Disbanded
1st Princess Louise's (Argyll & Sutherland Highlanders)	The Argyll & Sutherland Highlanders
2nd Gordon Highlanders	The Gordon Highlanders
2nd Princess Louise's (Argyll & Sutherland Highlanders)	The Argyll & Sutherland Highlanders
2nd Connaught Rangers	Disbanded

141

Name at Formation	Title Changes Infantry
95th Regt	Derbyshire
96th Regt	None
97th Regt	Earl of Ulster's
98th Regt	None
99th Regt	Lanarkshire
100th Regt	Prince of Wales' Royal Canadians
101st Regt	Royal Bengal Fusiliers
102nd Regt	Royal Madras
103rd Regt	Royal Bombay
104th Regt	2nd Bengal Fusiliers
105th Regt	2nd Madras Light Inf.
106th Regt	2nd Bombay Light Inf.
107th Regt	3rd Bengal Inf.
108th Regt	3rd Madras Light Inf.
109th Regt	3rd Bombay Light Inf.
Rifle Brigade (4 Battalions)	95th (Rifle Corps) Regt

1915 Title	Present Title
2nd Sherwood Foresters (Derbyshire)	The Sherwood Foresters
2nd Manchester	The King's Regt
2nd Queen's Own (Royal W. Kent)	The Queen's Regt
2nd Prince of Wales' (N. Staff.)	The Staffordshire Regt
2nd Duke of Edinburgh's (Wilts.)	The Duke of Edinburgh's Royal Regt
1st Prince of Wales (Leinster Royal Canadians)	Disbanded
1st Royal Munster Fusiliers	Disbanded
1st Royal Dublin Fusiliers	Disbanded
2nd Royal Dublin Fusiliers	Disbanded
2nd Royal Munster Fusiliers	Disbanded
2nd King's Own (Yorks. Light Inf.)	Light Inf.
2nd Durham Light Inf.	Disbanded
2nd Royal Sussex	The Queen's Regt
2nd Royal Inniskilling Fusiliers	Royal Irish Rangers
2nd Prince of Wales' Leinster (Royal Canadians)	Disbanded
Prince Consort's Own	Royal Green Jackets

The above listed regimental numbers and designations have evolved through the years by some volunteer regiments being amalgamated with others, or as the UK's forces become decimated, being completely disbanded, with only their colours and uniforms languishing in a military museum as solemn evidence that they ever existed. It is only in their medals that they really come alive again when the ever-enquiring collector starts to unfurl their medal rolls to reveal deeds of bravery and valour.

11 cleaning and presentation of medals

Once the collection reaches around the dozen mark the problem of suitable presentation arises. Many collectors house their medals in a ready-made cabinet comprised of thin, tray-like drawers lined with green baize upon which their treasured pieces are spread in fine array. Although this is handy for the collector faced with a space shortage it always seems a pity to me to have to hide a good collection away and to go through the performance of unlocking drawers, etc., before one can peruse each new acquisition. In this day and age of ever increasing thefts of fine antiques, paintings, weapons, figures and almost anything which can be sold to an unsuspecting dealer abroad, it behoves one to be a little security-minded, especially if the house or flat has to be left unattended for too long a period.

One of the most effective and picturesque· ways of displaying war medals is to mount them behind glass, rather in the manner of a picture. The backing can be either black, red or green velvet, according to individual taste.* With the many and various combinations of ribbon colours the background does play an important part in this form of display. Once again this will entirely depend on what format the collection takes; be it a collection of Victorian 'Heads' or the numerous world-wide battle groups.

Frames can either be made to a specific size or failing this a search around the local second-hand shops will usually turn up something just as good.

* Glued to a stiff backing of peg-board, ceiling-board or plywood.

If the picture frame method of display is to be used the medals must be affixed to the backing by any of the following examples. Nothing is worse than to have a good collection of EF to Unc medals shaken off their backing (when somebody slams a door!) and scattered all around the room.

Peg-board is by far the favourite as it can be purchased with holes punched 1in. or $\frac{1}{2}$in. apart. This makes it much easier to sew the ribbons to the velvet and then through into the holes behind. Press pins can be used of course in all instances but unless you purchase the all-brass pin your medals are liable to get rust marks on the ribbon from the inferior brass-coated variety. If you do decide to use press pins be sure to mount the medal in the following manner. Failure to do so makes for an unsightly pin-head on all the ribbons displayed.

Take each medal to be displayed and lay it in position. Now, gently flip it upon its back stretching the medal out to its full length of ribbon. Press in the pin about $\frac{1}{2}$in. from the ribbon end and then return the medal to its proper position by bringing the ribbon right over the pin-head thus concealing it from view.

For a much safer, neater and more professional touch I think the method of sewing them through the velvet and onto the peg-board is by far the most effective. Once the medals are correctly affixed and the small identification labels installed, finish off by pasting a piece of thick brown paper over the back of the frame. This combats the ever present danger of dust filtering in through the rear and damaging both ribbons and medals.

Next we come to the all-important task of cleaning. So many collectors spoil their medals by polishing or buffing them up with metal polish. This may be quite satisfactory on the brass or cupro-nickel medals struck for World War II; in fact this is all one can do with them for unlike their solid silver counter-parts of World War I and earlier, these cupro-nickel awards cannot be dipped in silver dip; but continual rubbing and polishing of the solid silver medals will, in time, reduce them to pieces of polished silver with all their intricate details and highspots reduced to a faceless nonentity.

For the best results when using silver dip, clean in the following manner. Carefully remove the ribbon and place it in between the pages of a heavy book. This ensures that the ribbon is out of harm's way as well as acting as a press. When one is handling a ribbon of say, 1870 it pays to be extra careful as in some instances the ribbon is harder to acquire than the actual medal!

Now, having stored your ribbon away safely take the medal to be dipped and thread a thin loop of nylon fishing line through the bar or suspender fitting, then thoroughly immerse the medal in the fluid. If two or more are to be cleaned pop them all in at one go leaving the loops of nylon cord hooked over the side of the jar. A word of warning here! If the medals are heavily tarnished be sure to carry out the above operation in a well ventilated room . . . better still in the workshop or garage – toxic fumes play havoc with the lungs! Once the dipped medal takes on a nice brilliant shine rinse it well in warm soapy water and after drying on a soft piece of towelling, lightly polish with a long term silver cloth.

Ribbons can prove a little bit of a problem especially if they are of any great age. Many of those struck at the turn of the century prove no trouble to replace but those of say, Germany 1939–45 or any pre-1860 types are next to impossible. For these very old ribbons the only thing to do is to lightly press with a warm iron using brown paper as a barrier – better a tatty, frayed antique ribbon than no ribbon at all!

abbreviations

Unc	– Uncirculated	DSO	– Distinguished Service Order
EF	– Extremely Fine		
NEF	– Nearly Extremely Fine	DSC	– Distinguished Service Cross
VF	– Very Fine	DFC	– Distinguished Flying Cross
GF	– Good Fine		
F	– Fine	AFC	– Air Force Cross
Av	– Average	DCM	- Distinguished Conduct Medal
AF	– As Found		
Diam	– Diameter	CGM	– Conspicuous Gallantry Medal
Ex	– Excellent		
F & G	– Framed & Glazed	DFM	– Distinguished Flying Medal
Msg	– Missing		
Mtd	– Mounted	AFM	– Air Force Medal
Mil	– Military	NGS	– Naval General Service
Obv	– Obverse	MGS	– Military General Service
Rev	– Reverse	IGS	– India General Service
Orig	– Original	GSM	– General Service Medal
Ov	– Overall		
QSA	– Queen Victoria South Africa Medal	BWM	– British War Medal (1914–20)
		VM	– Victory Medal
KSA	– King Edward VII South Africa Medal	ISM	– India Service Medal
Vol	– Volunteer	LS & GC	– Long Service & Good Conduct
WW I & II	– World Wars I & II		
		DSM	– Distinguished Service Medal
Wt	– Weight		
MM	– Military Medal	OBE	– Order of the British Empire
GC	– George Cross		
MC	– Military Cross		

bibliography

AUGUSTUS STEWARD, W., *The ABC of War Medals and Decorations.* Stanley Paul and Co., London, 1918

DORLING, H. and GUILLE *Ribbons and Medals.* George Philip and Son Ltd, London, 1963

ERLAM, Denys *Ranks and Uniforms of the German Army, Navy and Air Force.* Seeley Service and Co. Ltd, London

GRAMBERG, R. C., Ed. *Collectors' Handbook of German Military Relics.* Colortone Enterprises, USA

HIERONYMUSSEN, P., *Orders, Medals and Decorations of Britain and Europe in Colour.* Blandford Press, London, 1967

LAFFIN, J., *British Campaign Medals.* Abelard, London

MERICKA, V., *Orders and Decorations.* Paul Hamlyn, Middlesex, 1967

MOLLO, Andrew, *Uniforms of the SS, vol. I and II.* Historical Research Unit, 1968

POULSOM, N. W., *Catalogue of Campaign and Independence Medals.* Corbitt and Hunter, Newcastle

PURVES, A. A., *Collecting Medals and Decorations.* Seaby, London, 1968

SANTORO, Cesare,   *Hitler's Germany.* Internationaler
                       Verlag, Berlin, 1938

SMYTH, Sir John,   *Story of the Victoria Cross, 1856–64.*
                       Frederick Muller, London

WILKINS, P. A.,   *History of the Victoria Cross.* 1904

FISCHER, Karl,   *Waffen Technischer Leitfaden Für
                       Ordnungspolizei.* 1941

HETTLER, Eberhard,   *Uniformen Der Deutschen Wehrmacht.*
                       NSDAP

REIBERT, Dr W.,   *Der Deinst-Unterricht im Heere.* Mittler
                       und Sohn, 1942

Miscellaneous
publications: *British Orders and Awards.* Kaye and
                       Ward, London, 1969

                       Jarbuch des Deutschen Heeres. Verlag
                       von Breitkopf und Hartel, Leipzig, 1936

                       Deutschland Erwache. Bilderdienst
                       Ultona, Bahrenfeld, 1933

                       Adolf Hitler. Bilderdienst Hamburg,
                       Bahrenfeld, 1936

index

151